SRA
Reading
Mastery
Signature Edition

Workbook B

Siegfried Engelmann
Susan Hanner

SRA

A Division of The McGraw-Hill Companies
Columbus, OH

Illustration Credits
Rick Cooley, Heidi King, Simon Galkin,
Dan Schofield, Jim Shough, and Jessica Stanley

SRAonline.com

 SRA

A Division of The McGraw-Hill Companies

Printed in the United States of America.

Send all inquiries to this address:
SRA/McGraw-Hill
4400 Easton Commons
Columbus, OH 43219

ISBN: 978-0-07-612585-2
MHID: 0-07-612585-8

7 8 9 10 11 HES 13 12 11 10

The **McGraw·Hill** Companies

Name _____

A

1. When you teach an animal a simple trick, when do you reward the animal?

   _____

2. When don't you reward the animal?

   _____

3. Let's say that you want to teach an animal a very hard trick. Can the animal do the trick at first? _____

4. What will happen if the animal doesn't receive any rewards until it does the trick? _____

5. When you're teaching the animal a hard trick, what do you reward the animal for doing? _____

> Let's say you're training a dog to jump up in the air and do a backward somersault. **Use the words below to finish each sentence.**
>
> - jumping up and turning upside down
> - jumping up in the air
> - jumping up and leaning backward
>
> 6. At first you would reward the dog for _____
>
>   _____.
>
> 7. Later you would reward the dog for _____
>
>   _____.
>
> 8. Later you would reward the dog for _____
>
>   _____.

B Story Items

9. What's the name of the pet shop owner? _____

10. Why wasn't the pet shop making money? _____

_____

11. When Waldo let the cats out of their cages, what did Maria think the cats

    would do? _____

12. Did the cats do that? _____

13. What did they do? _____

_____

14. After Waldo let all the animals out of their cages, where did he sit down?

_____

15. Which animals did he feed first? _____

16. What was happening outside the pet shop window?

_____

GO TO PART D IN YOUR TEXTBOOK.

Name _____

A Story Items

1. How many pets did Maria usually sell in a week? _____

2. How many did she sell on the day that Waldo cooked? _____

3. Why did she sell so many more pets when Waldo cooked?

_____

4. Maria said that she would give Waldo some money for every dollar she

makes by selling pets. How much money? _____

5. How did Waldo feel about that deal? _____

6. When Waldo got home, he was out of breath. Tell why.

_____

7. Why was he late? _____

_____

8. Waldo changed his plans about cooking in the garage. Where will he cook?

_____

9. Did his parents like that idea? _____

10. Did Waldo know a lot about training animals? _____

11. How will he learn about training animals? _____

_____

12. What will he use as a reward when he trains animals? _____

_____

B Review Items

13. In which direction do geese migrate in the fall? _____

14. In which direction do geese migrate in the spring? _____

15. Write the directions **north, south, east** and **west** in the boxes.

16. Make a line that starts at the circle on the map and goes north.

17. If you start at the circle and move to the number 4, in which direction do

    you go? _____

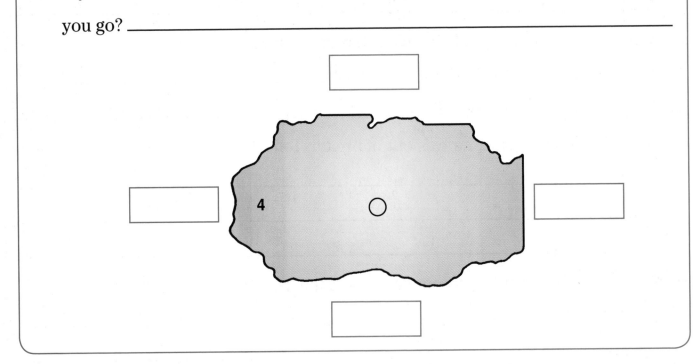

18. **Fill in the blanks to show the four seasons.**

    winter, _____, summer, fall, _____

    spring, _____, _____.

GO TO PART C IN YOUR TEXTBOOK.

Name _____

Ⓐ

1. Where did Waldo get books about training animals? _____

2. What kind of animals are the easiest to teach? _____

3. What did Waldo train three pigeons to do? _____

4. How long did it take the first pigeon to learn that trick? _____

5. Did it take **more time** or **less time** to train the second pigeon?

    _____

6. What did Waldo attach to the pigeon's feet? _____

7. Why did he do that? _____

8. Where did Waldo put the pigeons after he finished training them?

    _____

9. Why did he do that? _____

10. Maria didn't sell the first three pigeons that Waldo trained. Why not?

    _____

11. How many dancing pigeons did people order the first day? _____

12. Waldo trained a rabbit to walk on a tightrope. Where did he put the ropes at

    first? _____

13. What kind of ropes were they? _____

14. When Waldo put the ropes a few centimeters above the table, he did

    something so the rabbit wouldn't fall. What did he do? _____

    _____

15. What did Waldo do to make a super trick? _____

    _____

B Review Items

16. How many Great Lakes are there? _____

17. Color the Great Lakes on the map.

Here's the rule about an electric eye: **Each time the beam of light is broken, the light changes.**

18. The light is off. The beam is broken 5 times. Is the light **on** or **off** at the end?

_____

19. The light is off. The beam is broken 7 times. Is the light **on** or **off** at the end?

_____

20. The light is off. The beam is broken 2 times. Is the light **on** or **off** at the end?

_____

GO TO PART C IN YOUR TEXTBOOK.

Name ____________________

A Story Items

1. Where will the animal show take place? ____________________
2. On what day of the week will it be held? ____________________
3. At what time will it start? ____________________
4. How much is the admission? ____________________
5. Name **3** acts that will be in the animal show.

____

____

6. The more water the glass has, the ______ the sound it makes.

• higher • lower

7. **Cross out** the glass that will make the **highest** ring.
8. **Circle** the glass that will make the **lowest** ring.

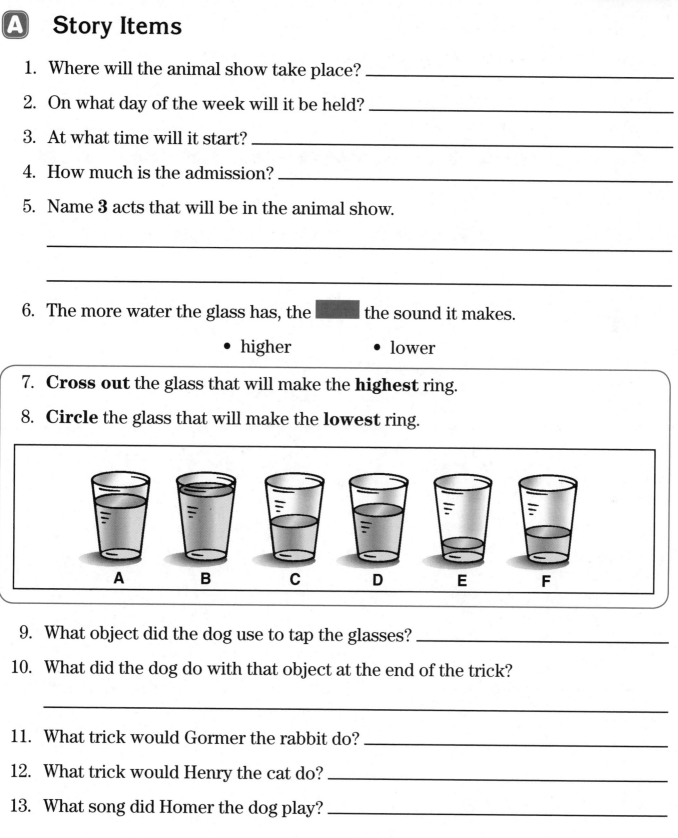

9. What object did the dog use to tap the glasses? ____________________
10. What did the dog do with that object at the end of the trick?

____

11. What trick would Gormer the rabbit do? ____________________
12. What trick would Henry the cat do? ____________________
13. What song did Homer the dog play? ____________________

14. Waldo and Maria decided to cook the food for the show at the high school.

   Why didn't they want to cook it at the pet shop? _____

   _____

15. Why wasn't Waldo able to cook his food at the high school?

   _____

16. What food will they use for rewards? _____

B Review Item

17. Draw arrows at **D**, at **E** and at **F** to show the way the melted rock moves.

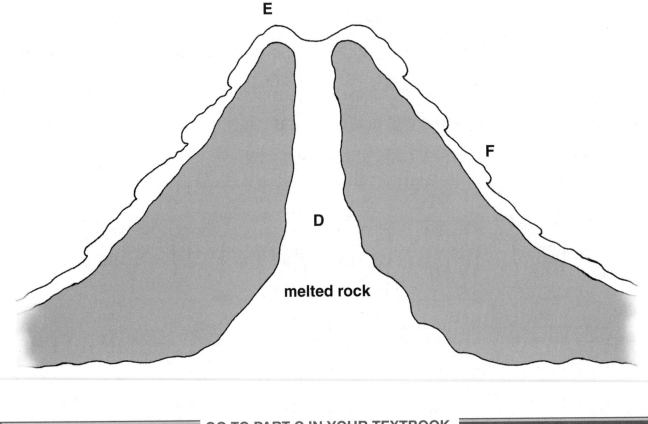

GO TO PART C IN YOUR TEXTBOOK.

Name _____

A Skill Items

east   attorney
north   million
muff   inventors
Mercury hundred
admission off
Venus   liquid
funnel   rocket
thousand walrus
museum
manufacturers

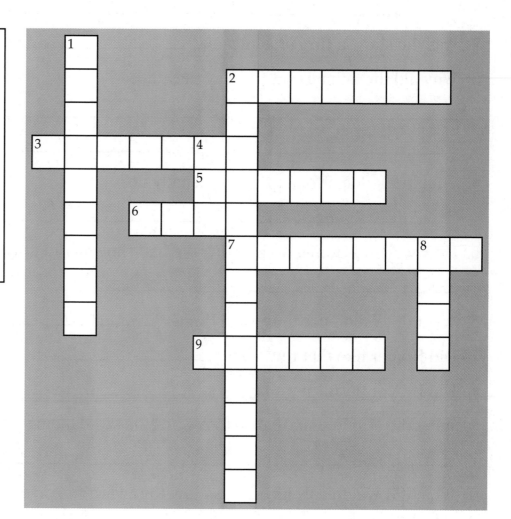

Across

2. A planet that is close to the sun is ▩.

3. A word for a **thousand thousands** is a ▩.

5. A whirlpool is shaped like a ▩.

6. Something you can wear over your ear to keep it warm is an ear ▩.

7. Another word for **lawyer** is ▩.

9. A place that has many different kinds of exhibits is called a ▩.

Down

1. The amount you pay to get into a show is called the ▩.

2. Inventors usually try to find ▩ to make their products.

4. If something is not turned **on,** it is turned ▩.

8. **West** is the opposite direction of ▩.

B Story Items

1. About how many people came to see the animal show?

   _____

2. Was the show a **flop** or a **success**? _____

3. Why did the animals act the way they did?

   _____

   _____

4. What trick does Homer the dog usually do?

   _____

5. How well did Homer do his trick the first time he did it in the show?

   _____

6. What did Waldo use to reward Homer? _____

7. Did Homer like that reward? _____

8. Did Homer perform well again? _____

9. What did Waldo **usually** use to reward the tap-dancing pigeons?

   _____

10. What did Waldo use during the show to reward the pigeons?

    _____

11. Did the pigeons keep doing their trick for that reward? _____

GO TO PART C IN YOUR TEXTBOOK.

Name _____

A Skill Items

overboard	ordinary
Alaska	usual
Florida	parents
stomach	restless
common	city
snow	state
Canada	country
oxygen	blister
sore	

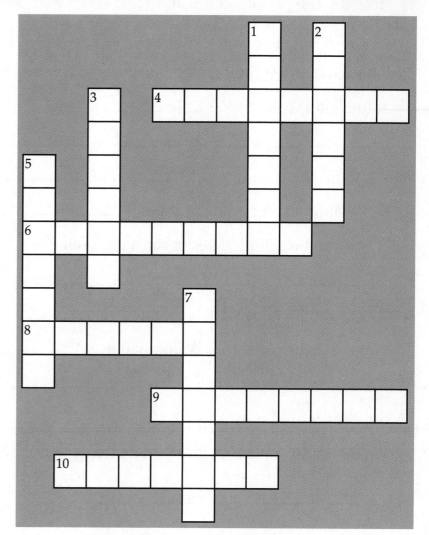

Across

4. Things you see all the time in different places are ▨ things.

6. When things go over the side of a ship, they go ▨ .

8. Geese that are gray and black and white are called ▨ geese.

9. When you feel ▨ , you don't want to keep doing what you're doing.

10. Japan is a ▨ .

Down

1. You may get a ▨ on your foot if your shoe doesn't fit well.

2. Oomoo and Oolak lived in the state of ▨ .

3. When Wendy was on Io, she had to wear an ▨ tank so she could breathe.

5. If you are hungry, your ▨ may make noise.

7. Your mother and father are called your ▨ .

Lesson 76 **11**

B) Story Items

1. How did the people in the audience feel about the animal show?

   _____

2. People returned their trained animals to the pet shop. Why wouldn't those

   animals do their tricks? _____

   _____

3. What did the people want? _____

4. Did Waldo eat very much dinner? _____

5. What was he thinking about during dinner?

   _____

6. Where did he go right after dinner? _____

7. Waldo's father said that Waldo had a _____ problem.

8. The animals would work for _____

   but they would not work for _____.

9. Waldo could solve this problem by training the animals to work for

   _____.

GO TO PART C IN YOUR TEXTBOOK.

Name _____

A Skill Items

flocks
Saturn
tune
reward
herds
incredible
green
audience
brown
Mercury
chant
experience
terrific
Jupiter
disturb
hitch

Across

4. Another word for **amazing** is ▮.

6. Geese live in large groups called ▮.

8. Each thing you do is an ▮.

9. Io is a moon of the planet ▮.

10. Another word for **bother** is ▮.

Down

1. The people who watch an event are called the ▮.

2. Here's another way of saying **He will tie the dog to the sled: He will** ▮ **the dog to the sled.**

3. Another word for **a song** is a ▮.

5. Jupiter is orange, white and ▮.

7. Something you get for doing a good job is a ▮ for doing that job.

Lesson 77   **13**

B   Story Items

1. Waldo read until late at night and then went to bed. Why didn't he go to sleep right away? _____

_____

2. When you teach animals to work for new rewards, do you change the reward **quickly** or **slowly?** _____

3. When you teach an animal to work for a new reward, what kind of reward do you start with? _____

4. Then what do you do to that reward? _____

_____

5. When do you stop changing the reward? _____

_____

6. What reward do Waldo's animals work for? _____

7. When Waldo teaches his animals to work for new rewards, what reward will he start with? _____

8. Then what will he do to that reward? _____

9. How long did the school day seem to Waldo? _____

10. Where did he go right after school? _____

11. What did he start doing as soon as he got there?

_____

GO TO PART C IN YOUR TEXTBOOK.

Name _____

A Story Items

Fill in each blank with the word **regular** or the word **coated.**

1. Waldo trained the pigeons to work for a new reward. First Waldo rewarded the pigeons with his special food. Next, Waldo rewarded the pigeons with

   two _____ seeds.

2. Next, Waldo rewarded the pigeons with two _____

   seeds and one _____ seed.

3. Next, Waldo rewarded the pigeons with two _____

   seeds and one _____ seed.

4. At the end, Waldo rewarded the pigeons with three _____ seeds.

5. Waldo trained the rabbit to work for a new reward. First, Waldo rewarded the rabbit with his special food. Next, Waldo rewarded the rabbit with two

   pieces of _____ carrots.

6. Next, Waldo rewarded the rabbit with two pieces of _____

   carrots and one piece of _____ carrot.

7. At the end, Waldo rewarded the rabbit with three pieces of

   _____ carrots.

8. Which people did Maria call after Waldo retrained the animals?

   _____

9. What did she tell those people about the animals?

   _____

Fill in each blank with the word **top** or the word **bottom.**

10. A **regular pyramid** has one animal at the _____ of the pyramid.

11. An **upside-down pyramid** has one animal at the _____ of the pyramid.

B Skill Items

truck
kayak
pole
boring
crater
Canada
Alaska
volcano
intelligent
drifting
equator
clever
hotter
ignore
colder
earthquake
automobile

Across

5. Another word for **car** is ▢ .

6. Most wild geese are born in ▢ .

7. **Interesting** is the opposite of ▢ .

9. The part of the earth that receives more heat than any other part is the ▢ .

Down

1. When an ice chunk is being moved by a current, we say that the ice chunk is ▢ .

2. A mountain that erupts is called a ▢ .

3. The kind of boat that Eskimos use is a ▢ .

4. The farther you go from the equator, the ▢ it gets.

6. Another word for **very smart** is ▢ .

8. When you don't pay attention to something you ▢ that thing.

GO TO PART C IN YOUR TEXTBOOK.

Name _____

A Story Items

1. In what country are the states of Colorado and Utah? _____

2. Name the mountains you drive over to get from Colorado to Utah.

   _____

3. In which direction do you go to get from Colorado to Utah? _____

4. Name 2 cities in Colorado. _____

5. Name one city in Utah. _____

6. Write **north, south, east** and **west** in the correct boxes.
7. Make an **R** on the state of Colorado.
8. Make a **T** on the state of Utah.

B Story Items

9. What animal was at the bottom of the upside-down pyramid?

   _____

10. Which dog stood on the huge dog's rear end? _____

11. Which dog stood with its paws on the huge dog's head? _____

12. How many cats were in the pyramid? _____

13. What animals did the cats stand on? _____

14. How many squirrels were in the pyramid? _____

15. What animals did the squirrels stand on? _____

16. How many pigeons were in the pyramid? _____

17. What animals did the pigeons stand on? _____

18. Waldo and Maria didn't show the upside-down pyramid before the animal

    show. Why not? _____

    _____

19. How many times did the dancing pigeons do their act? _____

20. How well did they do their act? _____

    _____

21. How did the audience respond to the dancing pigeons? _____

    _____

22. What did the audience do while Homer played "Mary Had a Little Lamb"?

    _____

    _____

GO TO PART D IN YOUR TEXTBOOK.

Name _____

A Story Items

1. When the animals did the super trick at Samson High School, what did the birds do before they landed on the squirrels? _____

2. How did Waldo signal the birds to land on the squirrels?

_____

3. How did the audience feel about the pyramid act?

_____

4. Some people put in special orders for trained animals. Name one of those special orders. _____

_____

5. What time of year is usually the busiest for the pet shop? _____

6. Did the pet shop have **more business** or **less business** than it had at Christmas? _____

7. What's a tour? _____

8. How long would Waldo's tour last? _____

9. How many shows is Maria planning for the tour? _____

10. How will Waldo keep up with his school work while he's on the tour?

_____

11. What will Waldo and Maria ride in when they travel from city to city?

_____

12. What will the animals travel in? _____

13. Who will drive? _____

14. Before Waldo could go, he would need _____ from his parents.

B Skill Items

involve	lower	Triceratops	gravity	tire	shortly
Rocky	higher	Tyrannosaurus	selected	regular	waste
contacted	clever	information	hire	deserve	

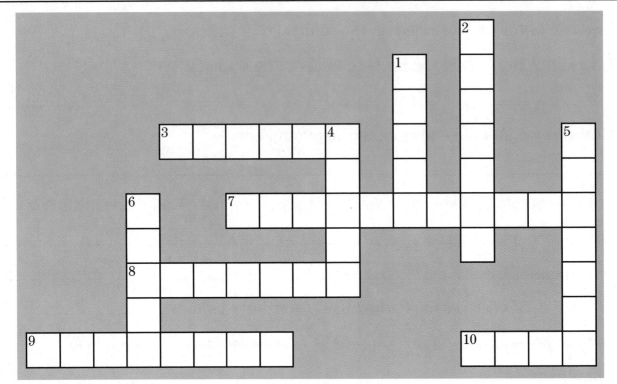

Across

3. Another word for **very smart** is ▮.

7. The name of the dinosaur that had horns and armor was ▮.

8. Another word for **soon** is ▮.

9. Another word for **chose** is ▮.

10. When you give someone a job, you ▮ that person.

Down

1. The more water the glass has, the ▮ the sound it makes.

2. Bigger planets have more ▮ than smaller planets.

4. To get from Colorado to Utah, you cross the ▮ Mountains.

5. Something you should receive is something you ▮.

6. When we use something the wrong way, we ▮ that thing.

GO TO PART C IN YOUR TEXTBOOK.

Name _____

Ⓐ Story Items

1. Who did Waldo's father want to talk to before he gave Waldo permission to go on the tour? _____

2. What did Waldo's father think after he talked to Maria?

   _____

3. How many shows did Waldo and Maria do **before** they got to Denver? _____

4. Which city did Waldo and Maria go to **after** Denver? _____

5. Which brakes stopped working first—the truck brakes or the trailer brakes?

   _____

6. Where was the truck when the brakes failed? _____

- Write **B** in front of each thing that happened **before** the tour.
- Write **D** in front of each thing that happened **during** the tour.

7. _____ The driver hooked up the line for the trailer brakes.

8. _____ Waldo saw a mountain goat.

9. _____ Waldo's parents gave permission for Waldo to go on the trip.

10. _____ The driver explained why the trailer needed brakes.

11. _____ Maria and Waldo stopped studying and looked at the mountains.

12. _____ Waldo and Maria did a show in Denver, Colorado.

13. _____ Waldo and Maria did a show at Samson High School.

14. How did the truck engine sound to Waldo at the end of the story?

    _____

15. What did Waldo smell at the end of the story? _____

Lesson 82   **21**

B Review Items

Look at the picture.

16. Shade the part of the earth where it is nighttime.

17. Which side of the earth is closer to
    the sun, J or K? _____

18. Which side of the earth is in
    nighttime? _____

19. Which side of the earth is in
    daytime? _____

K

J

Sun

20. Write **north, south, east** and **west** in the correct boxes.

21. In which direction is ocean current **L** moving? _____

22. In which direction is ocean current **M** moving? _____

23. Which direction is the
    wind coming from?

    _____

24. Make an arrow above ice
    chunk **N** to show the
    direction the current will
    move the ice chunk.

25. Make an arrow above ice
    chunk **P** to show the
    direction the current will
    move the ice chunk.

L   N

P

M

GO TO PART C IN YOUR TEXTBOOK.

Name _____

A Story Items

1. Why couldn't the driver stop the truck? _____

_____

2. How many pounds of weight do you have to push down with to make the

emergency brake work? _____

3. If the huge dog had **all** its weight on the brake, would the brake work?

_____

4. Did the huge dog weigh **more than 100 pounds** or **less than 100 pounds?**

_____

5. How many paws did the huge dog have on the brake? _____

6. Was the weight of the three dogs enough to make the brake work? _____

7. Was that enough weight to make the brake stop the trailer very fast? _____

8. Why was it important for the trailer to stop fast? _____

_____

9. What did Waldo do to get more weight on the brake?

_____

_____

B Review Items

10. Write the names of the 9 planets, starting with the planet closest to the sun.

_____

_____

Lesson 83   **23**

11. In which direction do geese migrate in the fall? _____

12. In which direction do geese migrate in the spring? _____

13. Write the directions **north, south, east** and **west** in the boxes.

14. Make a line that starts at the circle on the map and goes north.

15. If you start at the circle and move to the number 5, in which direction do

   you go? _____

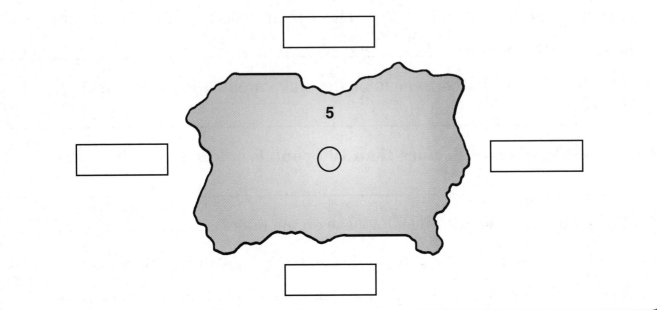

16. How many moons does Jupiter have? _____

17. How many moons does Saturn have? _____

18. Which planet has more moons, Saturn or Jupiter? _____

19. How far is it from Earth to Jupiter? _____

20. Do gases surround Io? _____

21. How much oxygen is on Io? _____

GO TO PART C IN YOUR TEXTBOOK.

Name _____

A

Write the name of each kind of coral below the correct picture.

- **red coral**   - **staghorn coral**   - **brain coral**

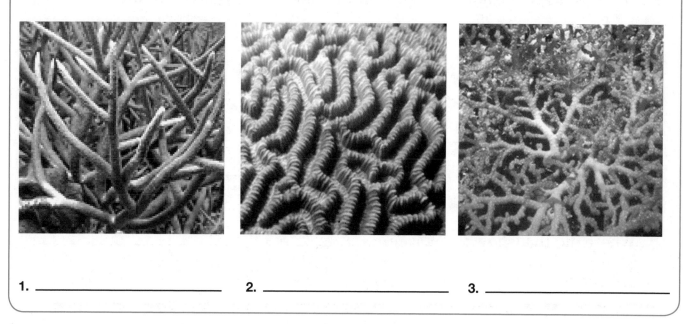

1. _____   2. _____   3. _____

4. Coral is made up of the _____ of tiny _____.

5. An underwater hill that is covered with coral is called a coral _____.

6. Where do the animals that make up a coral reef spend their whole life?
- all over the ocean   - in one place

B Story Items

7. The weight of three dogs and four cats was on the emergency brake.

   Was that more than 80 pounds? _____

8. Was that enough weight to stop the truck? _____

9. To keep the brake locked in place, the driver turned _____.

10. After the truck had stopped, what treat did Waldo give the animals?

    _____

11. Why did he give them a treat? _____

    _____

12. What trick did the animals do for the people who gathered around the

    truck? _____

13. How long did it take to get the brakes fixed? _____

14. Where did the truck and trailer go after the brakes were fixed?

    _____

15. What followed the truck and trailer? _____

16. Waldo remembered one show as the greatest show his animals ever did.

    Where did that show take place? _____

    _____

C Skill Items

Here are 3 events that happened in the story. Write **beginning, middle** or **end** for each event.

17. The show in Utah was a great success. _____

18. The truck was at the curve now, but it was hardly moving. _____

19. Two other policemen were directing traffic around the truck and trailer.

    _____

GO TO PART D IN YOUR TEXTBOOK.

Name _____

Ⓐ Story Items

1. What was Darla deathly afraid of? _____

2. Name 2 things Darla wasn't afraid of. _____

   _____

3. How would Darla feel when water got up to her neck?

   _____

4. Name 2 acts of bravery. _____

   _____

5. Complete the rule about being brave. To be brave, you must _____

   _____.

6. Was holding snakes an act of bravery for Darla? _____

7. Tell why. _____

   _____

8. Was swimming an act of bravery for Darla? _____

9. Tell why. _____

   _____

10. Where was Darla going to take swimming lessons? _____

    _____

11. What sign did Darla have to show that she became frightened when she

    thought about swimming? _____

B Review Items

12. Write the missing seasons on the picture below.

13. Shade half of earth **R** and half of earth **T**.

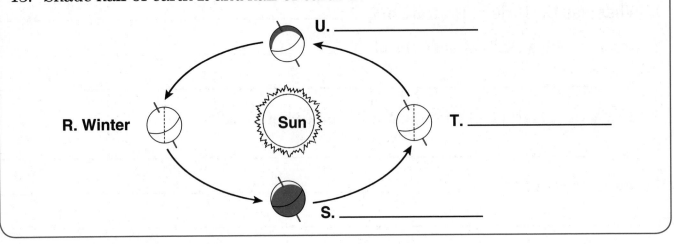

U. _____

R. Winter

Sun

T. _____

S. _____

14. Which uses more oxygen, running or sitting? _____

15. What's another name for hot, melted rock? _____

GO TO PART C IN YOUR TEXTBOOK.

Name _____

86

A

1. When you dive down 33 feet, you have _____ times the pressure on you that you have at the surface.

2. When you dive down 66 feet, you have _____ times the pressure on you that you have at the surface.

Write the missing numbers in the blanks.

0 feet	surface pressure
3. _____ feet	2 times surface pressure
4. _____ feet	3 times surface pressure
5. _____ feet	4 times surface pressure

6. Write the letter of the body that has the **least** pressure on it. _____

7. Write the letter of the body that has the **most** pressure on it. _____

8. Write the letters of all the bodies that have **more** pressure on them than **D** has on it. _____

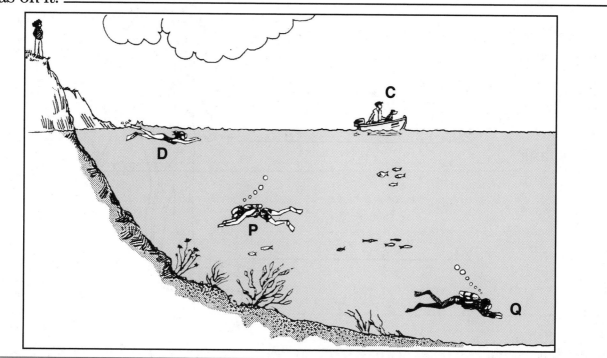

B Story Items

9. What does the color of water tell you about the water?

_____

10. Name **2** things Darla did when she was learning to swim.

_____

_____

11. What was Darla getting ready to do in this story? _____

_____

12. What problem did Darla have with her scuba mask the first time she tried to

wear it? _____

13. How did she **feel** when that happened? _____

14. What was the deepest dive Darla had ever made? _____

15. How deep will she dive this time? _____

Label these parts of the scuba equipment.

16. _____

17. _____

- air hose
- mouthpiece
- fins
- mask
- dial
- air tank
- wet suit

18. _____

19. _____

20. _____

22. _____

21. _____

GO TO PART D IN YOUR TEXTBOOK.

Name _____

A Story Items

1. The diving boat was about _____ miles east of the United States.

2. Name the islands that are near the place they are diving.

   _____

3. Were the divers **north** or **south** of those islands?_____

4. In what ocean are they diving? _____

5. What did the guide tell the divers to do if they got separated?

   _____

6. How deep were the divers at the end of the story? _____

7. How deep are the divers going to go? _____

8. If you go underwater that deep, the pressure is much greater than it is on

   land. How many times greater is it? _____

9. When divers are that deep, how long should they take to return to the

   surface of the water? _____

10. What may happen to the divers if they go up faster than that?

    _____

11. What made Darla's ears hurt? _____

    _____

12. How deep was she when they started to hurt? _____

13. If you move up too fast from very deep water, you may get the _____.

14. What forms in your blood as you go up too fast? _____

15. When you go up very fast, is there **more pressure** or **less pressure** on your

    body? _____

Lesson 87   **31**

Fill in the blanks to show how deep the divers would be.

16. When the diver is _____ feet underwater, the pressure is two times as great as it is on land.

17. When the diver is _____ feet underwater, the pressure is three times as great as it is on land.

18. When the diver is _____ feet underwater, the pressure is four times as great as it is on land.

19. Could Darla feel the weight of her air tank underwater? _____

20. Could Darla feel the pressure of the water? _____

21. Name **2** things that were part of the incredible scene that Darla and Julie saw. _____

22. When Darla looked at the other divers below her, what did she think they looked like? _____

23. What happened each time a diver breathed? _____

_____

24. What did the diving guide point out to the group? _____

_____

25. When you open a bottle of soda pop, what happens to the pressure inside the bottle? _____

26. What forms in the soda pop? _____

GO TO PART C IN YOUR TEXTBOOK.

Name _____

Ⓐ Story Items

1. How deep did the divers go? _____

2. About how long did it take them to get there? _____

3. Did things look **darker** or **lighter** at the bottom? _____

4. There weren't as many plants down there because there wasn't as much

    _____

5. Name **3** things the great water pressure was doing to Darla.

    _____

    _____

6. Why did the bubbles following the divers look dark gray?

    _____

7. What is the name of the arrow-shaped fish that Darla saw?

    _____

8. Write **2** facts Darla knew about these fish.

    _____

    _____

9. Is the water cooler at **100 feet down** or **at the surface?**

    _____

10. Is all the water at 100 feet down the same temperature? _____

11. What should a diver's bubbles look like? _____

12. What did Julie's bubbles look like? _____

13. What did that mean? _____

    _____

14. Julie started to go to the surface very fast. Why did Darla want to catch

Julie? _____

_____

15. Who could swim faster, Darla or Julie? _____

Answer these questions about a buoyancy device:

16. What do you fill it with? _____

17. When it is filled up, what happens to the diver? _____

_____

18. When it is empty, what happens to the diver? _____

_____

19. What hard decision did Darla have to make after she caught up with Julie?

_____

20. What did Darla decide to do? _____

_____

21. Did Julie want to share the air hose with Darla? _____

22. Julie didn't know what she was doing because she was in a state of

_____

GO TO PART C IN YOUR TEXTBOOK.

Name _____

A

1. In what state is the Iditarod sled-dog race? _____

2. In which city does it begin? _____

3. In which city does it end? _____

4. The Iditarod is about ▮▮▮ miles from start to finish.

   - 500   - 1100   - 1600 miles

5. In most years, the race takes about ▮▮▮.

   - a week   - 10 days   - 2 weeks

6. The person who drives a sled-dog team is called a _____.

7. The drivers of the sled-dog teams command the dogs by using their ▮▮▮.

   - reins   - steering wheels   - voices

B Story Items

8. As Darla and Julie moved up to the surface of the water, they had to stop ten feet below the surface. How long did they wait there?

   _____

9. Why didn't the girls go straight up to the surface? _____

   _____

10. How did the water pressure change as the girls moved toward the surface?

    _____

11. How did the light around them change as they moved toward the surface?

    _____

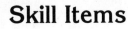

Skill Items

coral	overcome	Colorado	understand	emergency	instructor
bends	reef	California	surface	buoyant	suffer
oxygen	Utah	bare	success	bubbles	musher

Across

2. Another word for **teacher** is ▨.

4. When you solve a problem, you ▨ the problem.

6. A brake you use if the regular brake doesn't work is called an ▨ brake.

8. When you open a bottle of soda pop, ▨ form in the pop.

10. One of the states in the western part of the United States is ▨.

Down

1. When you do very well at something, you have ▨.

3. An underwater hill that's covered with coral is called a coral ▨.

5. The person who drives a sled-dog team is called a ▨.

7. ▨ is made up of the shells of tiny animals.

9. If divers move up too fast from very deep water, they may get the ▨.

GO TO PART D IN YOUR TEXTBOOK.

Name _____

A

1. Most sled-dog teams have an ▮▮▮▮ number of dogs.
   - even   • odd

2. For the Iditarod, a sled-dog team can't have more than _____ dogs.

---

3. Which letter shows the swing dogs? _____

4. Which letter shows the wheel dogs? _____

5. Which letter shows the lead dogs? _____

6. Which letter shows where the musher is most of the time? _____

7. Which letter shows the gang line? _____

8. Which letter shows tug lines? _____

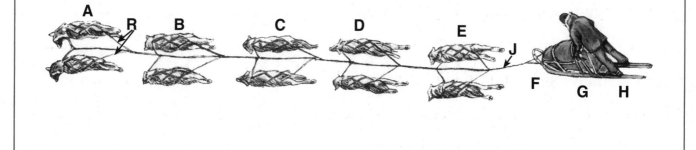

Use these words to answer items 9–11:

• **wheel dogs**   • **lead dogs**   • **swing dogs**

9. These dogs are responsible for freeing the sled when it gets stuck.

_____

10. These dogs are very smart, and other dogs obey them.

_____

11. These dogs are very good followers, and they are smart.

_____

B Story Items

12. What town does Susie live near? _____

13. In what state does she live? _____

14. What's the name of her dog? _____

15. Susie's Uncle Chad was getting ready for _____

16. Susie went to Chad's place on a _____

17. What kind of sled dog was Susie's dog? _____

18. Was he going to be part of Chad's regular sled-dog team? _____

19. How many times had Chad entered the Iditarod before? _____

20. How many times had he finished the race at Nome? _____

21. What was his goal for the Iditarod this year?

_____

22. This year's race would begin in a little more than _____ weeks.

23. Chad drove the dogs and his sled to ▇▇▇.
    • Eagle Claw Valley   • Beaver River Valley   • Eagle River Valley

24. Chad wanted to find out what the team would do in really ▇▇▇.
    • cold weather   • rough country   • flat country

GO TO PART D IN YOUR TEXTBOOK.

Name _____

Ⓐ

1. What do sled dogs wear to protect their feet? _____

2. **Underline** the 4 items that tell what could happen to a sled dog's feet if they didn't have protection.
   - snowballs between the pads
   - slipping on hard snow
   - stiff legs
   - icicles on their ankles
   - cuts from ice and frozen snow
   - long claws
   - cuts that do not heal well

3. The booties that Chad prefers are made of _____

4. If booties are too tight, what could happen? _____

   _____

5. If booties are too loose, what could happen? _____

   _____

Ⓑ Story Items

6. How many dogs did Chad plan to run in the Iditarod? _____

7. How many dogs did Chad start with at Eagle River Valley? _____

8. How many dogs did Susie keep on leashes? _____

9. Why did Chad put bags of dirt on the sled? _____

   _____

10. The dogs wore something they didn't usually wear for practice runs. What

    was that? _____

11. Why did they wear them for this run? _____

    _____

12. What command tells sled dogs to turn left? _____

13. What command tells them to turn right? _____

14. What command tells them to move straight ahead? _____

15. What did Chad do to test the dogs?

 • He got the sled stuck against rocks.   • He ran the dogs along the road.

 • He did not tell the dogs what to do.

Review Items

16. Write **north, south, east** and **west** in the correct boxes.

17. In which direction is ocean current **B** moving? _____

18. In which direction is ocean current **C** moving? _____

19. Which direction is the wind coming from? _____

20. Make an arrow above ice chunk **D** to show the direction the current will move the chunk.

21. Make an arrow next to ice chunk **E** to show the direction the current will move the chunk.

GO TO PART D IN YOUR TEXTBOOK.

Name _____

A Story Items

1. To get the sled free, Chad first gave commands to the _____ dogs.

2. When the sled tipped over, the dogs on leashes thought Chad was ▮▮▮▮.
   - awkward
   - playing
   - angry

3. Why didn't some of the dogs on the gang line run over to Chad?

   _____

4. During most of the practice, how many dogs were on the gang line?

   _____

5. At the end of the practice, how many dogs were on the gang line?

   _____

6. Which number of dogs was easier to handle? _____

7. Which number of dogs made a more powerful team? _____

8. When were the dogs going to be examined?

   _____

9. What happens if a dog does not pass the examination? _____

   _____

B Skill Items

avoid	strain	barracuda	booties	shark
leash	gang	left	gee	lead
tug	swing	haw	wheel	mush
Alaska	Nome	equator	Anchorage	purpose

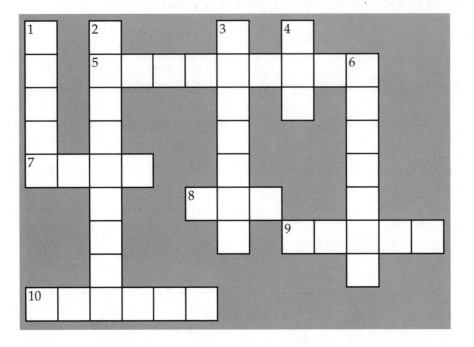

Across

5. The city where the Iditarod begins is ▇▇▇.

7. The ▇▇▇ dogs on a sled-dog team are very smart, and other dogs obey them.

8. The command that tells sled dogs to turn right is ▇▇▇.

9. When you stay away from something, you ▇▇▇ that thing.

10. The Iditarod is held in the state of ▇▇▇.

Down

1. The ▇▇▇ dogs on a sled-dog team are responsible for freeing the sled when it gets stuck.

2. An arrow-shaped fish is a ▇▇▇.

3. Sled dogs wear ▇▇▇ to protect their feet.

4. The command that tells sled dogs to turn left is ▇▇▇.

6. The make-believe line around the middle of the earth is called the ▇▇▇.

GO TO PART C IN YOUR TEXTBOOK.

Name _____

Ⓐ Story Items

1. At the beginning of today's story, who was late in the morning?

   _____

2. Susie was surprised to see which dog in the truck? _____

3. Chad told Susie that he planned to run _____ dogs.

4. How did that make Susie feel? _____

5. Which 2 dogs would now be on the team?

   _____

6. What does a musher have to do with any dogs that are injured during the

   Iditarod? _____

7. What did Chad plan to do with some dogs if he had trouble with a team

   of sixteen? _____

8. According to the rules, there must be at least how many dogs on the gang

   line at the end of the Iditarod? _____

9. The veterinarian found out that one dog had a problem. Which dog?

   _____

10. What was the problem? _____

11. What job does that dog have on Chad's team? _____

B Review Items

Write the missing numbers in the blanks.

	feet	surface pressure
	___0___ feet	surface pressure
12.	_____ feet	2 times surface pressure
13.	_____ feet	3 times surface pressure
14.	_____ feet	4 times surface pressure

15. Write the missing seasons on the picture below.

16. Shade half of earth **W** and half of earth **Y**.

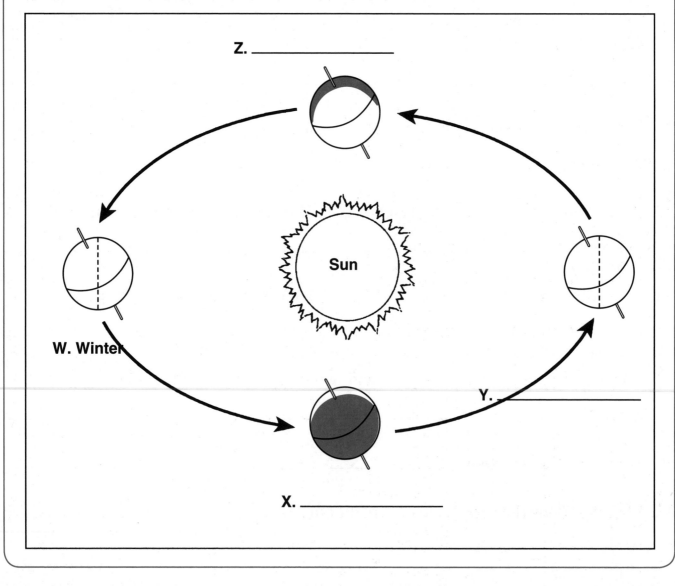

Z. _____

Sun

W. Winter

Y. _____

X. _____

Name _____

A

1. The rules for the Iditarod require the musher to have certain things. **Underline** those things.

- enough food for a day
- firewood
- an ax
- enough food for a week
- extra shoes
- booties
- a tent
- a good sleeping bag
- snowshoes
- extra dogs

2. How much food does each dog need every day?

- 3 pounds
- 2 pounds
- 1 pound

3. The sled must have room to hold ████.

- another musher
- an injured dog
- a spare sled

B **Story Items**

4. What did Chad decide to do with Chugger? _____

5. He gave some reasons for his decision. **Underline** 2 reasons.
- She had always been the fastest runner.
- She had never had any hip problems.
- She was frequently sick.
- Neither of her parents had hip problems.
- She was only three years old.

6. What's the name of the woman whose picture was on Susie's wall?

_____

7. How many times did she enter the Iditarod? _____

8. How many times did she finish in first place? _____

9. On March 15, what was the weather like when the race began?

_____

10. How many mushers start the race at the same time?

                 • 1   • 2   • 10   • all

11. How much time passes before the next musher starts? _____

12. What number was Chad? _____

13. The musher in front of Chad was from _____.

14. When mushers are on the trail, how much help can they get from someone

     else? _____

Review Items

Look at the picture below.

15. Shade the part of the earth where it is nighttime.

16. Which side of the earth is closer to the sun, **W** or **X?** _____

17. Which side of the earth is in nighttime? _____

18. Which side of the earth is in daytime? _____

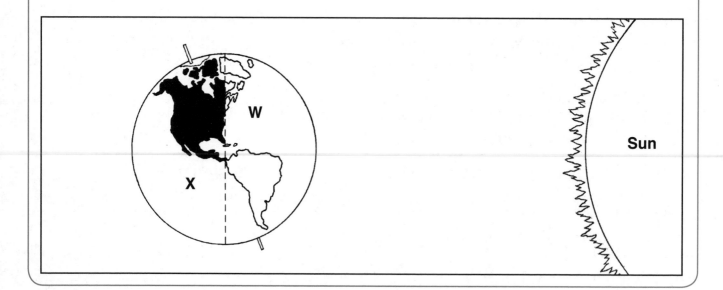

GO TO PART D IN YOUR TEXTBOOK.

Name _____

A

1. Why are checkpoints called checkpoints? _____

_____

2. Name **3** things a musher does at checkpoints.

_____

_____

_____

3. How does food get to the checkpoints?

_____

4. About how far apart are the checkpoints? _____

5. About how many checkpoints are there between Anchorage and Nome?

_____

B Story Items

6. Just before Chad left, Susie became worried. What worried her?

_____

7. Was Chad **calm** or **nervous?** _____

8. What was the name of the woman who left just before Chad?

_____

9. How do mushers get water for their dogs? _____

_____

10. What do mushers often use to make beds for their dogs?

_____

11. **Underline** the items that tell what it was like on the third day of the race.
- frozen lakes
- 10 degrees below zero
- rough country
- hard, icy snow
- blowing snow
- soft snow
- blasting wind
- flat trail
- mountains
- warm
- sunny
- 10 degrees above zero

12. What was the name of the pass Chad was going through?

_____

13. Why did he think that name was funny? _____

_____

14. What's the name of the first woman to win the Iditarod?

_____

15. In what year did she win it? _____

16. Where were she and most of the mushers when the race was stopped the

first time? _____

17. Why did Susie write a different letter after she heard the TV report?

_____

18. In the letter she didn't send, what did she write about? _____

_____

19. What did the race officials think they would have to do if the bad weather

continued? _____

GO TO PART D IN YOUR TEXTBOOK.

Name _____

A   Story Items

1. Would the snow be deeper **on the trail** or **off the trail?** _____

2. Why? _____

3. If Chad had stayed on the trail, he would have gone in which direction?

   _____

4. How did he figure out which direction he was going? _____

   _____

5. Did he turn **left** or **right** in order to go in the correct direction? _____

6. When the wind finally died down, how much daylight was there?

   _____

7. What could Chad see? _____

8. How did the dogs know they were near the checkpoint? _____

   _____

9. How did they act? _____

10. When Chad arrived at the lodge, how many mushers were missing? _____

11. What was the name of one of those mushers? _____

12. How did Chad show the officials the route he had taken?

    _____

13. When did Chad see one of the missing mushers? _____

    _____

Esther	Mars	Pluto	Venus	thorough	complete	veterinarian
vocabulary	Riddles	fierce	doctor	Susan	test	examination
Butcher	Iditarod	sixteen	fifteen	Libby	cruel	

Across

3. All the words a person knows is called the person's ▬▬▬.

4. Another word for **animal doctor** is ▬▬▬.

6. The last name of the first woman to win the Iditarod is ▬▬▬.

8. The first name of the woman who finished the Iditarod sixteen times is ▬▬▬.

9. Another word for **checkup** is ▬▬▬.

Down

1. Something is ▬▬▬ if it doesn't overlook anything.

2. Another word for **very wild** is ▬▬▬.

3. The planet that's between Mercury and Earth is ▬▬▬.

5. A great sled-dog race that's held in Alaska every year is called the ▬▬▬.

7. How many dogs are allowed on a team in the Iditarod?

GO TO PART C IN YOUR TEXTBOOK.

Name _____

A

1. The rules of the Iditarod state that every musher must rest for _____ hours at one checkpoint and must rest for _____ hours at two other checkpoints.

2. This rule was put in to protect the [____].
   - mushers   - dogs   - race officials

3. In what year was the first Iditarod?   - 1973   - 1963   - 1993

4. During the first running of the Iditarod, how many dogs died during the race?   - 10   - 20   - 30

5. During more recent years, how many dogs die during each race?
   - 5 to 8   - 8 to 10   - 2 to 3

B Story Items

6. Write **3** on the map to show where Chad was on day 3.
7. Write **9** on the map to show where he was on day 9.

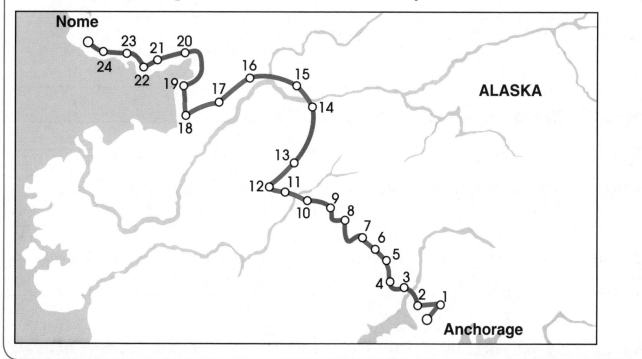

Lesson 98   **51**

8. Something was the same on day 3 of the race and day 9 of the race. What was that? _____

_____

9. What happened as the sled was going over a thick crust of frozen snow?

_____

10. Which dog let out a yelp? _____

11. Chad was in the water up to his _____ .

12. Name the 2 dogs that had to do most of the pulling to get the sled out of the

water. _____

13. What did Chad do with the tarp? _____

14. What did Chad do first, take care of the injured dog or take care of himself?

_____

15. How much time did he have to get dry and warm?

_____

16. What would have happened if he took too much time? _____

_____

17. Name **3** things he did inside the tent that he built.

_____

_____

_____

18. What did Chad do to find the trail? _____

19. Whose sled did he see? _____

20. When he harnessed the dogs, which 2 dogs were the wheel dogs?

_____

21. Which dog walked behind the sled? _____

22. Where was Chugger? _____

GO TO PART D IN YOUR TEXTBOOK.

Name _____

A Story Items

1. Where did Chad leave Chugger before going on to finish the race?

   _____

2. How many dogs were now on the gang line? _____

3. Which dog did not have a partner? _____

4. Chad finished the race in _____ th place.

5. Siri Carlson finished in _____ th place.

6. Did Chad meet his main goal for this race? _____

7. What was that goal? _____

8. How did the mushers and their teams get back to Anchorage from Nome?

   _____

9. Who met Chad at the airport? _____

10. Susie had a lot of questions. Most of them were about _____ .

11. What had the vet told her the day before about Chugger? _____

   _____

12. What did Chad say he wanted to do with Denali for the next Iditarod?

   _____

13. Who did Chad plan to practice with during the summer? _____

14. Denali ran in six more Iditarods. Who was the musher for five of them?

   _____

15. Who was the other musher? _____

B Review Items

16. Most sled-dog teams have an ▓▓▓ number of dogs.   • even   • odd

17. For the Iditarod, a sled-dog team can't have more than _____ dogs.

18. Which letter in the picture shows the wheel dogs? _____

19. Which letter shows the swing dogs? _____

20. Which letter shows the lead dogs? _____

21. Which letter shows where the musher is most of the time? _____

22. Which letter shows tug lines? _____

23. Which letter shows the gang line? _____

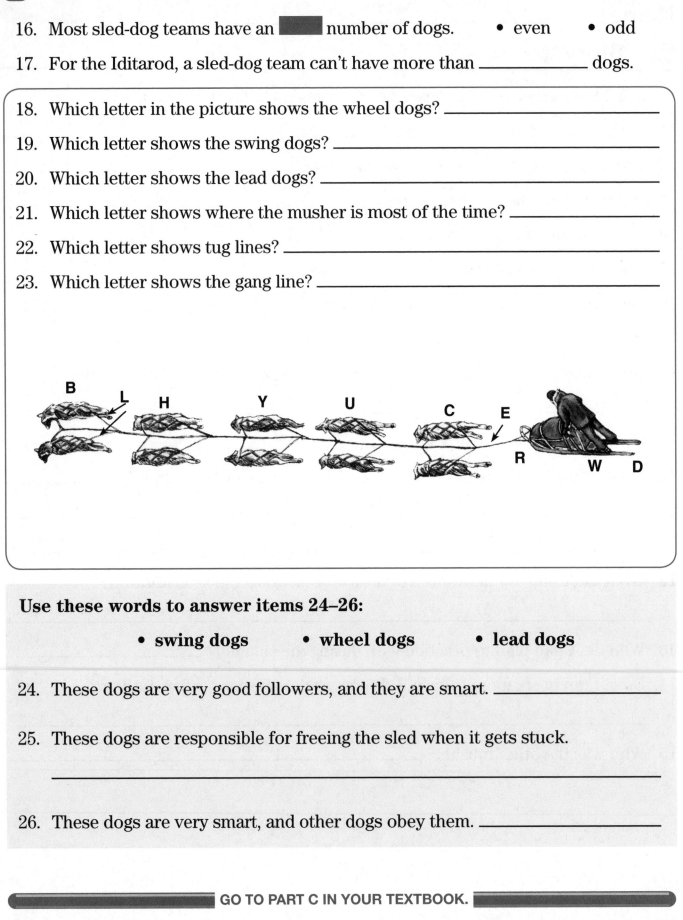

Use these words to answer items 24–26:

   • **swing dogs**   • **wheel dogs**   • **lead dogs**

24. These dogs are very good followers, and they are smart. _____

25. These dogs are responsible for freeing the sled when it gets stuck.

_____

26. These dogs are very smart, and other dogs obey them. _____

GO TO PART C IN YOUR TEXTBOOK.

Name _____

A Story Items

1. In which month does this story take place? _____

2. Was Al happy about the test he had taken in school? _____

3. Did Al like school very much? _____

4. What did the sign in the store window say?

   _____

5. Who owned the store? _____

6. Does Al need money to pay for the trips the old man will take him on?

   _____

7. What does Al have to do to pay for his trips?

   _____

8. For Al's first trip, he wanted to go in a _____ because he

   liked to go _____.

9. What will happen if Al passes a test the old man gives him?

   _____

10. What will happen if Al doesn't pass a test? _____

    _____

B Skill Items

chilly	sick	inventor	problem	electricity	need	invent
shopkeeper	pale	patent	manufacturers	invention	warm	

Across

1. When you invent something, you start with a ▩ .

4. Businesses that make things are called ▩ .

5. The object that an inventor makes is called an ▩ .

6. An inventor gets a ▩ to protect an invention.

7. Another word for **sort of cold** is ▩ .

Down

2. Leonard's invention ran on ▩ .

3. The person who makes an object for the first time is called an ▩ .

6. When people look whiter than they usually look, the people look ▩ .

GO TO PART C IN YOUR TEXTBOOK.

Name _____

A

1. How far does light travel in one second?
   - 86 miles
   - 186 thousand miles
   - 186 miles

2. What else travels as fast as light? _____

3. How long does it take light to travel from the sun to Earth?

   _____

B Story Items

4. What does Al have to do to pay for his trips?

   _____

5. Name the first vehicle Al and the old man rode in.

   _____

6. What was the fastest speed they went in that vehicle?
   - 500 miles per hour
   - 130 miles per hour
   - 200 miles per hour

7. Why did Al and the old man have to shout in the racing car?

   _____

8. Name the second vehicle Al and the old man rode in.

   _____

9. How fast did they go in that vehicle?

_____

10. If the speedometer needle on the red racer is pointing to 70, how **fast** is the vehicle going?

_____

11. How **far** will that vehicle go in one hour? _____

Review Items

12. Write the names of the 9 planets, starting with the planet that's closest to the sun.

_____

_____

_____

13. During the Iditarod, what does a musher have to do with any dogs that are injured?

_____

14. According to the Iditarod rules, there must be at least how many dogs on the gang line at the end of the race? _____

15. During the Iditarod, how much food does each dog need every day?
    - 1 pound
    - 2 pounds
    - 3 pounds

16. Each sled in the Iditarod must have room to hold ▇▇▇.
    - a spare sled
    - another musher
    - an injured dog

GO TO PART D IN YOUR TEXTBOOK.

Name _____

A **Story Items**

1. Why doesn't it feel like you're moving when you're speeding through space?

   _____

2. What is a cloud of stars called? _____

3. What will happen if Al passes the old man's test?

   _____

4. What will happen if Al doesn't pass the test?

   _____

5. Name the 3 vehicles Al and the old man rode in.

   _____

6. How long does it take sound to travel one mile? _____

7. How long did it take the jet plane to travel one mile?
   - less than 5 seconds   - 5 seconds   - more than 5 seconds

8. Why was it so quiet inside the jet plane?

   _____

9. How fast did they go in the last vehicle they were in?
   - 9 thousand miles per hour   - 9 thousand miles   - 4 thousand miles per hour

Look at the names of objects below.

10. Put a **1** next to the thing that travels the slowest.

11. Put a **2** next to the thing that travels the next slowest.

12. Number the rest of the objects to show how fast they travel.

    _____ rocket   _____ racing car   _____ jet plane   _____ light

Review Items

13. Write **north**, **south**, **east** and **west** in the correct boxes.

14. In which direction is ocean current **F** moving? _____

15. In which direction is ocean current **G** moving? _____

16. Which direction is the wind coming from? _____

17. Make an arrow above ice chunk **H** to show the direction the current will move the ice chunk.

18. Make an arrow next to ice chunk **I** to show the direction the current will move the ice chunk.

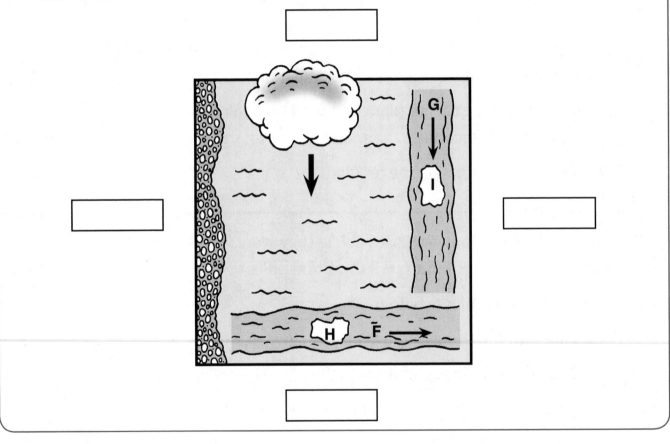

GO TO PART C IN YOUR TEXTBOOK.

Name _____

A Story Items

1. Al had trouble going to sleep because ▮▮▮▮.
   - he wasn't tired.
   - he kept thinking about his trip.
   - he was hungry.

2. Why did Al leave for school early?
   - to read the newspaper
   - to read his science book
   - to talk to his teacher

3. Why was Al's teacher surprised when he raised his hand in school?

   _____

4. It is so quiet in a jet plane that is going 900 miles per hour because the plane

   is moving faster than _____.

5. What was the name of the street the store was on?

   _____

6. What question did the old man ask Al?

   _____

7. Why did the old man say he would take Al on another trip?

   _____

8. What did Al want to learn about on his next trip? _____

9. Al's teacher had told the class that all things are made of _____.

10. How many forms of matter are there? _____

Review Items

11. Write the missing seasons on the picture below.

12. Shade half of earth D and half of earth F.

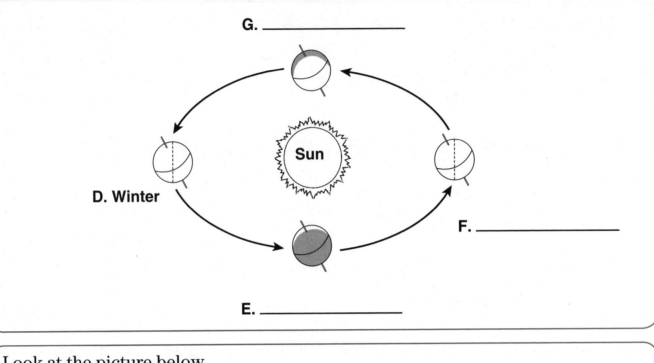

G. _____

D. Winter

F. _____

E. _____

Sun

Look at the picture below.

13. Which side of the earth is closer to the sun, P or Q? _____

14. Which side of the earth is in nighttime? _____

15. Which side of the earth is in daytime? _____

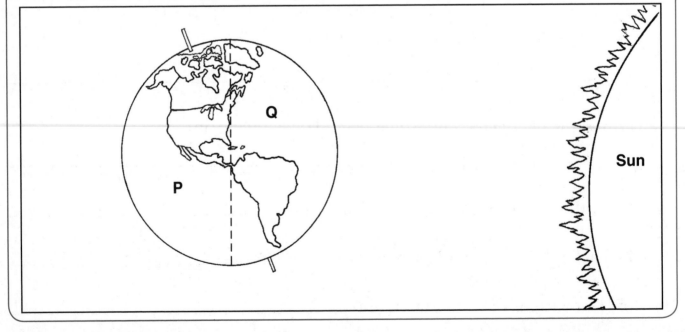

Q

P

Sun

GO TO PART C IN YOUR TEXTBOOK.

Name _____

A Story Items

1. When things are hard, what form of matter are they?

   _____

2. When hard matter gets hotter, which form does it change into first?

   _____

3. When matter gets still hotter, which form does it change into?

   _____

4. At first, the frying pan was matter in the _____ form.

5. How can you change a solid form of matter into a liquid?

   _____

6. To change a liquid form of matter into a gas, you make the liquid

   _____.

7. What is the coldest form of matter? _____

8. The sun is matter in the _____ form.

9. What form of matter is a rock? _____

10. What form of matter is the air around you? _____

11. What form of matter did the rock turn into when the old man let go of it?

   _____

12. Look at the list below. Put an **M** in front of everything that is matter.

_____ air   _____

_____ water   _____

_____ ice   _____

_____ brick   _____

_____ wood   _____

_____ steam   _____

_____ glass   _____

_____ tea   _____

_____ smoke   _____

_____ juice   _____

Look at the list above.

13. Write **solid** after everything that is matter in the solid form.

14. Write **liquid** after everything that is matter in the liquid form.

15. Write **gas** after everything that is matter in the gas form.

GO TO PART C IN YOUR TEXTBOOK.

Name _____

A Story Items

1. Al and the old man were on several planets with the bottle of air. On which planet did they fill the bottle with air? _____

2. Then Al and the old man took the bottle of air to a planet that has rings. Which planet was that? _____

3. Which planet did Al and the old man go to next? _____

4. In what form of matter is air on Saturn? _____

5. In what form of matter is air on Earth? _____

6. In what form of matter is air on Pluto? _____

7. Which planet is colder, Saturn or Pluto? _____

8. Why is that planet colder? _____

   _____

9. What form of matter is water? _____

10. What form of matter is steam? _____

11. What form of matter is ice? _____

12. How can you change a liquid form of matter into a solid?

    _____

13. How can you change a liquid form of matter into a gas?

    _____

14. What was strange about Anywhere Street?

    _____

15. How did Al feel about himself when he realized that he understood matter?

    _____

B Review Items

16. **Write the letters** of the 5 things that are matter in the solid form.

_____

17. **Write the letters** of the 4 things that are matter in the liquid form.

_____

18. **Write the letters** of the 3 things that are matter in the gas form.

_____

a. brick	d. juice	g. smoke	j. wood
b. glass	e. milk	h. tea	k. water
c. ice	f. rock	i. air	l. steam

19. The sun is matter in the _____ form.

20. What form of matter is the air around you? _____

GO TO PART C IN YOUR TEXTBOOK.

Name _____

A Story Items

1. Why didn't Al tell his mother he had gone to Saturn and Pluto?

   _____

2. Why did Al stay up so late?

   _____

3. What did Al do in school that showed he was very tired?

   _____

4. The old man asked Al two questions. Write one of those questions.

   _____

5. Why did the old man disappear from the store? _____

   _____

6. What is the hottest form of any matter? _____

7. What is the next-hottest form of any matter? _____

8. What is the coldest form of any matter? _____

9. Why didn't Al know the answers to the old man's questions?

   _____

10. What did the sign in the store window usually say?

    _____

11. What did the sign in the store window say after Al failed the test?

    _____

12. Where did Al go to find the answers to the questions the old man asked?

_____

13. Where did Al go after he left that place?

_____

14. Why did he go there? _____

_____

B Review Items

15. Draw arrows at **J,** at **K** and at **L** to show the way the melted rock moves.

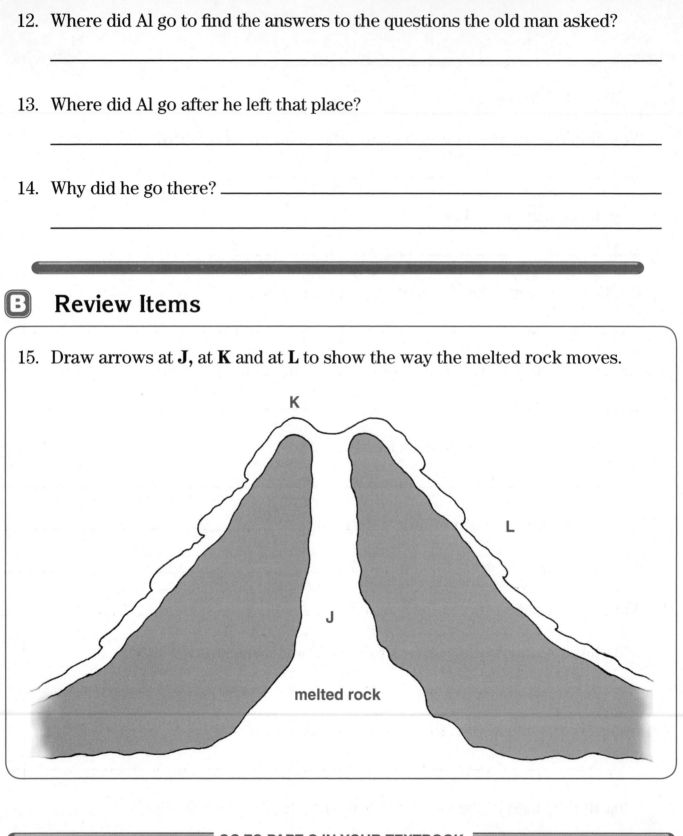

K

L

J

melted rock

GO TO PART C IN YOUR TEXTBOOK.

Name _____

A Story Items

1. Why did the old man give Al a harder test?

   _____

2. Did Al pass the harder test? _____

3. Do all things turn into a gas at the same temperature? _____

4. All matter is made up of _____.

5. After Al passed the test and left the store, what did the sign in the

   window say? _____

6. Do sugar molecules look like air molecules? _____

7. Do all sugar molecules look the same? _____

8. What did Al do that surprised his class? _____

   _____

9. What did Al want to see on his next trip? _____

10. Name 5 things that are made up of molecules. _____

    _____

11. Why can't you see molecules when you look at an object? _____

    _____

B Skill Items

Earth   binoculars

pressure   light

planets   stars

sun   Jupiter

Pluto   Saturn

moon   gravity

telescope   Io

sunshine   Mars

Neptune

Across

2. The sun gives heat and ▮▮▮ to all the planets.

5. The largest planet in the solar system is ▮▮▮.

7. The planet that is farthest from the sun is ▮▮▮.

8. One of Jupiter's moons is named ▮▮▮.

9. The planet we live on is called ▮▮▮.

Down

1. The force that makes things fall to the ground is ▮▮▮.

3. You can look through a ▮▮▮ to see some planets.

4. The ▮▮▮ is in the middle of the solar system.

6. There are nine ▮▮▮ in the solar system.

GO TO PART C IN YOUR TEXTBOOK.

Name _____

A Story Items

1. How did Al and the old man change to go inside the grain of sand?

   _____

2. The old man told Al, "A grain of sand is made of space and

   _____."

3. How were the sand molecules arranged? _____

4. The sand molecules that Al saw were in the _____ form of matter.

5. **Underline** 2 things that tell about any molecules in the solid form.
   - They fly around.
   - They stay in place.
   - They are hot.
   - They are lined up.

6. The old man planned to make the grain of sand colder than

   _____.

Review Items

Use these names to answer the questions: **Tyrannosaurus, Triceratops.**

7. What is animal G? _____

8. What is animal H? _____

Lesson 109 **71**

9. Name an arrow-shaped fish. _____

10. Write **2** facts about those fish. _____

    _____

11. Is the water cooler at **100 feet down** or **at the surface?**

    _____

12. Is all the water at 100 feet down the same temperature? _____

13. What do you fill a buoyancy device with?

    _____

14. When it is filled up, what happens to the diver?

    _____

15. When it is empty, what happens to the diver?

    _____

GO TO PART C IN YOUR TEXTBOOK.

Name _____

Ⓐ Story Items

1. How many globes were in each sand molecule? _____

2. How many tiny balls were in the center globe? _____

3. How can you make the molecules in a liquid move faster?

   • Heat them.   • Cool them.

4. How can you make the molecules in a liquid move slower?

   _____

5. When sand molecules are as cold as they can get, how much do they move?

   _____

6. Do they move **more** or move **less** at room temperature? _____

7. In which form of matter do molecules move fastest?

   _____

8. In which form of matter do molecules move slowest?

   _____

9. In which form of matter are molecules lined up in rows?

   _____

B

Triceratops	lava	Tyrannosaurus	whirlpools	storms
China	Mesozoic	Greece	mention	earthquake
blushed	glance	Tokyo	hesitated	suppose	dinosaurs

Across

3. Hot, melted rock is called ▮▮▮.

5. A huge killer dinosaur was named ▮▮▮.

6. Another word for **believe** or **think** is ▮▮▮.

7. When you look at something very quickly, you ▮▮▮ at the thing.

8. In the Bermuda Triangle, there are many ▮▮▮.

Down

1. Leonard ▮▮▮ when the audience applauded.

2. The animals that lived during the Mesozoic were called ▮▮▮.

4. The time when dinosaurs lived is called the ▮▮▮.

5. The largest city in Japan is ▮▮▮.

GO TO PART C IN YOUR TEXTBOOK.

Name _____

A Story Items

1. Al wanted to tell Angela his secret about Anywhere Street, but

   part of his mind told him that Angela _____

   _____.

2. Did she believe Al's story about the old man and the trips? _____

3. Did Angela believe that Al knew a lot about molecules? _____

4. Why did Al know so much about molecules? _____

   _____

5. Where did he go after school? _____

6. The old man gave Al a test on molecules. Write the 2 questions the old man
   asked. Then write the answers to the questions.

   Question 1: _____

   Answer 1: _____

   Question 2: _____

   Answer 2: _____

7. After the test, Al asked the old man a question. What did he want the old

   man to do? _____

8. How will Angela pay for her trip?

   _____

B Review Items

9. How many moons does Saturn have? _____

10. How many moons does Jupiter have? _____

11. How far is it from Earth to Jupiter? _____

seconds	seven	matter	solid	hours
molecules	answer	minutes	respond	cloud
liquid	galaxy	lava	gas	three

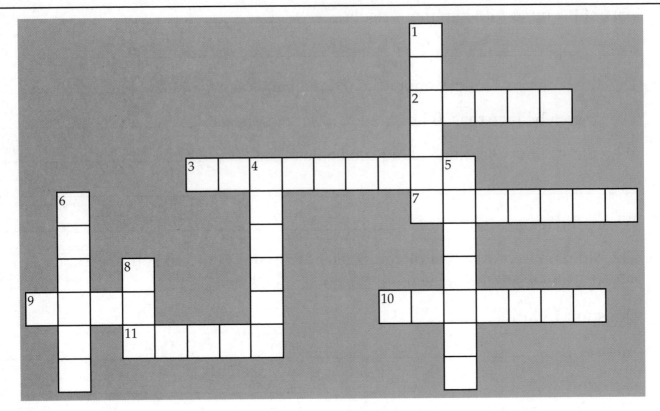

Across

2. There are ▨▨▨ forms of matter.

3. Tiny parts of matter are called ▨▨▨ .

7. Another word for **react** is ▨▨▨ .

9. Hot melted rock is ▨▨▨ .

10. It takes light 8 ▨▨▨ to travel from the sun to Earth.

11. When things are hard, they are matter in the ▨▨▨ form.

Down

1. Air, water and dirt are different forms of ▨▨▨ .

4. Water is matter in the ▨▨▨ form.

5. It takes sound 5 ▨▨▨ to travel one mile.

6. A cloud of stars is called a ▨▨▨ .

8. The air around you is matter in the ▨▨▨ form.

GO TO PART C IN YOUR TEXTBOOK.

Name _____

Ⓐ Story Items

1. After supper, Al said to Angela, "Let's go for a walk. I want to tell you something." What did he want to tell her?

   _____

2. Al kept making a picture of what Angela's face would look like when she found out that Al had been telling the truth. He imagined that her mouth

   would _____.

3. He imagined that her eyes would _____.

4. How did the picture that Al imagined compare to the one that he actually saw?

   _____

5. Was Angela surprised that there really was an Anywhere Street? _____

6. How did Angela feel when the old man first appeared?

   _____

7. Where did the old man take Al and Angela?

   _____

8. Why did Al take off his jacket and open his shirt?

   _____

9. What animal charged at Al and Angela?

   _____

B   Review Items

10. What do sled dogs wear to protect their feet? _____

11. **Underline the 4 items that tell what could happen to a sled dog's feet if they didn't have protection.**
    - a. slipping on hard snow
    - b. snowballs between the pads
    - c. icicles on their ankles
    - d. stiff legs
    - e. long claws
    - f. cuts that do not heal well
    - g. cuts from ice and frozen snow

12. If booties on a sled dog are too tight, what could happen?

    _____

13. If booties are too loose, what could happen?

    _____

14. What command tells sled dogs to turn right? _____

15. What command tells sled dogs to move straight ahead? _____

16. What command tells sled dogs to turn left? _____

17. During the Iditarod, what does a musher have to do with any dogs that are

    injured? _____

18. According to the Iditarod rules, there must be at least how many dogs

    on the gang line at the end of the race? _____

GO TO PART C IN YOUR TEXTBOOK.

A Story Items

1. What happened to the elephant that was chasing Angela?

    _____

2. Where did the old man take Al and Angela after they left the jungle?

    _____

3. Who wanted to go there? _____

4. How deep was the **bottom** of the ocean where Al and Angela were?

    - 200 feet
    - 2 miles
    - 20 feet

5. What covers some of the rocks? _____

6. What is coral made of?

    - animal shells
    - rocks
    - insects

7. When the old man blew up the balloon, it was about as big as

    _____ .

8. The old man stopped at 30 feet from the surface. As he went up, did the balloon have **more** or **less** air pressure on it? _____

9. So did the balloon get **bigger** or **smaller?** _____

10. Then what happened to the balloon?

    _____

11. Where would a balloon be bigger—at 60 feet below the surface or at 120 feet below the surface?

_____

Here's how big a balloon is at 20 meters below the surface.

Here's the same balloon when it is **deeper** or **not as deep.**

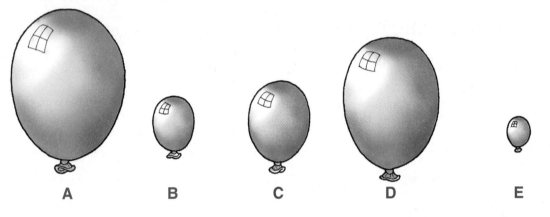

A   B   C   D   E

12. Write **D** on each balloon that is deeper than balloon **X.**

13. **Circle** the balloon that is the **deepest.**

14. **Cross out** the balloon that is **closest to the surface.**

15. What is the old man going to show Al and Angela next?

_____

16. How does Angela feel about that? _____

GO TO PART C IN YOUR TEXTBOOK.

Name _____

A Story Items

1. Al and Angela saw a huge whale. Name that whale.

   _____

2. The old man told Al and Angela, "The squid moves by

   _____."

3. Name the largest animal in the world. _____

4. That animal weighs more than _____ elephants.

5. Are whales fish? _____

6. What's the name of a smaller whale that is black and white?

   _____

7. Are whales **warm-blooded** or **cold-blooded?**

   _____

---

8. Name the animal in the picture. _____

9. Which arrow shows the way the animal squirts water out? _____

10. Which arrow shows the way the animal will move? _____

11. Make a **T** on a tentacle.

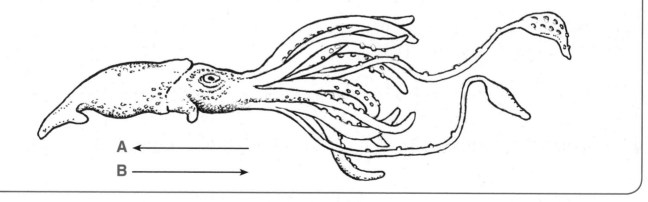

B Review Items

The picture shows marks left by an animal.

12. Which arrow shows the direction the animal is moving? _____

13. Write the letter of the part that shows the mark left by the animal's tail.

_____

14. Write the letter of the part that shows a footprint. _____

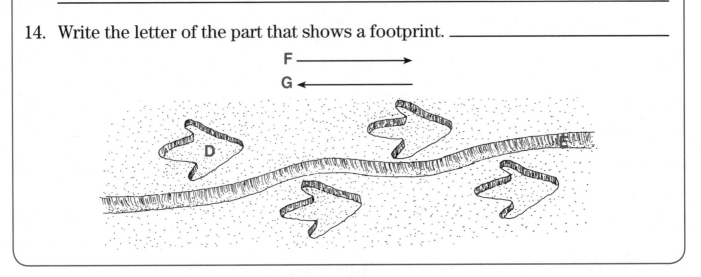

15. In which form of matter are molecules lined up in rows?

_____

16. In which form of matter do molecules move slowest?

_____

17. In which form of matter do molecules move fastest?

_____

18. Where would a balloon be bigger—at 90 feet below the surface
    or at 60 feet below the surface?

_____

GO TO PART C IN YOUR TEXTBOOK.

Name _____

Ⓐ Story Items

1. The old man made a high sound. What did that tell the killer whales to do?

   _____

2. Did the killer whales kill the blue whale? _____

3. How deep is the deepest part of the ocean?
   - 60 miles   - 10 miles   - 6 miles

4. Do plants grow on the bottom of the deepest part of the ocean? _____

5. Tell why. _____

6. Do the fish on the bottom of the ocean look like fish near the surface?

   _____

7. What is animal A? _____

8. What is animal B? _____

9. What is animal C? _____

A

B

C

10. When Al and Angela got home, their mother was holding a package. Who

    was the package from? _____

11. What was inside the package? _____

12. What was shown in the picture on the cover?

    _____

13. Some pictures in the book showed things that Al and Angela had seen on
    their trip. Name **2** of those things.

    _____

    _____

14. Where did Al take the book the next day? _____

15. Who made fun of Al in school? _____

16. How did the students in Al's class like his explanations of the things in the

    book? _____

17. What did the students do when Al finished his talk?

    _____

GO TO PART C IN YOUR TEXTBOOK.

Name _____

A **Story Items**

1. Where did Al and Angela go after school?

   _____

2. Why was Angela walking so fast?

   _____

3. The old man asked Al and Angela many questions about the sea. Write 2 of those questions. Then write the answers.

   Question 1: _____

   _____

   Answer 1: _____

   Question 2: _____

   _____

   Answer 2: _____

4. Where did Angela want to go on their next trip?

   _____

5. Name the first star that the old man showed Al and Angela.

   _____

6. Al and Angela saw flames on the sun that were _____ times bigger than Earth.

7. Al and Angela went to a little star. That star was _____ miles through the middle.

8. Earth is _____ miles through the middle.

9. Which weighs more, the little star or Earth? _____

10. The old man put a spoonful of matter on one side of the balance scale. What was the first thing he put on the other side of the scale?

_____

11. Did the scale balance? _____

12. What object finally made the scale balance?

_____

13. So the spoonful of matter weighed as much as 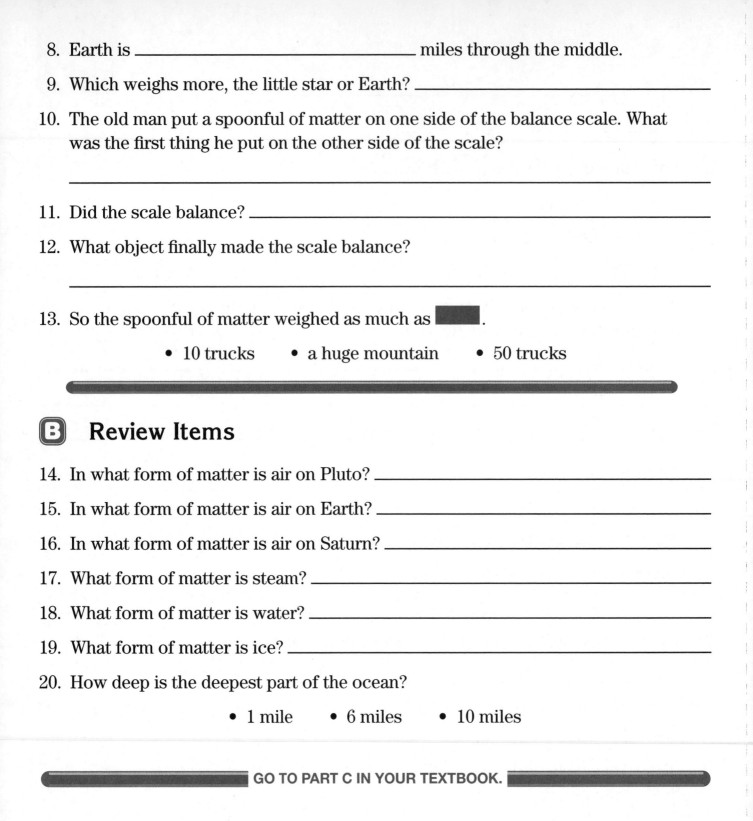 .

- 10 trucks   • a huge mountain   • 50 trucks

B Review Items

14. In what form of matter is air on Pluto? _____

15. In what form of matter is air on Earth? _____

16. In what form of matter is air on Saturn? _____

17. What form of matter is steam? _____

18. What form of matter is water? _____

19. What form of matter is ice? _____

20. How deep is the deepest part of the ocean?

- 1 mile   • 6 miles   • 10 miles

GO TO PART C IN YOUR TEXTBOOK.

Name _____

A Story Items

1. Is our sun a **huge** star? _____

2. Al and Angela went to a huge star. Name the planets that would be inside that star if it was in the center of our solar system.

   _____

   _____

3. How long would it take light to travel from one side of that star to the other

   side? _____

4. Name the galaxy that Al and Angela saw.

   _____

5. How many stars are in that galaxy?

   _____

6. How long does it take light to travel from one side of that galaxy
   to the other side?
   - 100 thousand years
   - 180 thousand years
   - 40 years

7. One star in the galaxy started flashing. What's special about that star?

   _____

Lesson 118   **87**

temperature	pressure	giant	blue	squid	killer
thousand	hundred	skeletons	shells	coral	plants
two	ten	selected	exclaimed	tentacles	

Across

4. Coral is made up of ▆▆▆ of sea animals.

7. ▆▆▆ whales are black and white.

8. The arms of a squid are called ▆▆▆.

9. A sea animal that looks like a giant carrot is a ▆▆▆.

10. The old man used a balloon to show Al and Angela how ▆▆▆ works.

Down

1. Earth is 8 ▆▆▆ miles through the middle.

2. The largest animal in the world is the ▆▆▆ whale.

3. Some rocks underwater are covered with ▆▆▆.

5. Another word for **chose** is ▆▆▆.

6. A blue whale weighs as much as ▆▆▆ elephants.

GO TO PART C IN YOUR TEXTBOOK.

Name _____

A Story Items

1. The teacher told the class that in two days they would have a test on

   _____ .

2. Was Al excited about the test? _____

3. Did Al want to learn about the human body? _____

4. As the man's arm pushed the weight overhead, the muscle on the back of
   the arm got ▮▮▮▮ .

   - shorter and thicker
   - longer and thicker
   - longer and thinner

5. Why were the store windows decorated? _____

   _____

6. Why did Al feel sad when he looked inside those windows?

   _____

   _____

7. What present did Al want to buy for his mother?

   _____

8. Who decided where to go on the next trip? _____

9. At the end of the story, what did the old man do to one of the muscles?

   _____

10. Name the muscle on the **front** of the upper arm. _____

11. Name the muscle on the **back** of the upper arm. _____

12. How many jobs does each muscle have? _____

13. Name the arm muscle that gets shorter when you straighten your arm.

_____

14. Name the arm muscle that gets shorter when you bend you arm.

_____

15. When you bend your arm, one of the muscles gets longer as the other one

gets shorter. Name the muscle that gets longer. _____

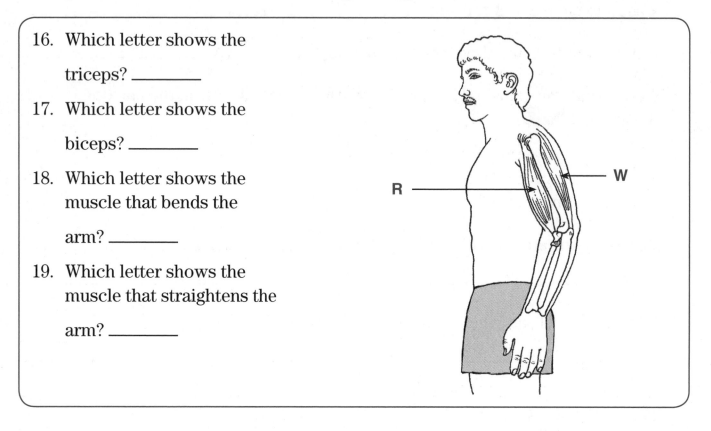

16. Which letter shows the triceps? _____

17. Which letter shows the biceps? _____

18. Which letter shows the muscle that bends the arm? _____

19. Which letter shows the muscle that straightens the arm? _____

GO TO PART C IN YOUR TEXTBOOK.

Name _____

A Story Items

1. Most muscles are attached to _____.

2. What happened when the old man removed the bones from the model's

   legs? _____

   _____

3. What is the skeleton of the human body made of?
   - bones   - skin   - muscles

4. How many bones are in the human body? _____

5. **Underline** the 2 things that bones do.
   - protect body parts
   - make the body move
   - get shorter and thicker
   - make the body strong

6. Did Angela like how the skeleton looked? _____

7. Name the bone on the top of the head. _____

8. What does that bone protect? _____

9. What would happen if something hit the **back** of your brain?

   _____

10. What would happen if something hit the **lower part** of your brain?

    _____

11. What **2** body parts do the ribs protect?

    _____

12. Your heart is about as big as your _____.

13. What might happen if something hurt your lungs?

_____

14. Does Al want to learn more about the body? _____

15. Had Al wanted to learn about the body before this trip started?

_____

16. At the end of the story, Al and Angela were inside a large tube that was

   filled with _____.

B Review Items

17. Name the largest planet in the solar system. _____

18. How long does it take Jupiter to spin around one time?

_____

19. How long does it take light to travel from the sun to Earth?

_____

20. Where would a balloon be bigger—at 40 feet below the surface of the ocean
   or at 80 feet below the surface?

_____

21. Are whales fish? _____

22. Are whales **warm-blooded** or **cold-blooded?**

_____

GO TO PART C IN YOUR TEXTBOOK.

Name _____

A Story Items

1. At the beginning of the story, Al and Angela were floating in a tube. What is that tube called? _____

2. Name the liquid that was in the tube. _____

3. What color was that liquid? _____

4. What was making the great pounding sound that Al and Angela heard?

   _____

5. Why was the pounding sound getting louder? _____

   _____

6. What happens to the blood when the heart pounds?

   _____

7. The old man told Al and Angela what the heart does. He told them that

   the heart _____ through the body.

8. What are the doors in the heart made of? _____

9. Which chamber of the heart was bigger, the first one or the second one?

   _____

10. How many doors were in the second chamber? _____

11. You can hear two sounds in the heart. The blood makes the little

    sound when it leaves the little _____.

12. When does it make the big sound?

    _____

13. When Al and Angela left the heart, they were in another blood vessel. What was different about how the blood moved in that blood vessel?
    - Things kept starting and stopping.
    - Things moved at the same speed.
    - Things moved very slowly.

14. Where was that blood vessel going?
    - from the body
    - to the heart
    - to the lungs

15. What does blood get in the lungs?
    - water
    - oxygen
    - food

16. Things can't burn without _____.

17. In the lungs, the color of the blood changed from _____

    to _____.

18. What color is blood that does not have oxygen? _____

19. What color is blood that has fresh oxygen? _____

GO TO PART C IN YOUR TEXTBOOK.

Name _____

A Story Items

1. When Angela and Al left the lungs, they were in a blood vessel. Where was the blood vessel going?

   _____

2. What color was the blood around them when they left the lungs?

   _____

3. Why was the blood that color? _____

   _____

4. How many chambers does the heart have? _____

5. How many chambers did Al and Angela go through **before** they went to the lungs? _____

6. How many chambers did they go through **after** they went to the lungs?

   _____

7. Where does black blood go after it leaves the heart?

   _____

8. Then the blood goes back to the _____.

9. Then the blood goes to the _____.

10. Why does oxygen blood have to go back to the heart after it leaves the

    lungs? _____

    _____

11. Muscles are made up of tiny _____.

12. When the oxygen left the blood, the color of the blood changed from

    _____ to _____.

13. Muscle cells need _____ to work.

Use these words to answer the questions below:
- blood vessels that lead from the heart
- blood vessels that lead to the heart

14. Which blood vessels pound every time the heart beats?

    _____

15. Which blood vessels do not pound?

    _____

16. Which blood vessels are blue?

    _____

17. Blood vessels that are blue are filled with _____ blood.

18. Did Angela want to take the trip around the body again? _____

19. Tell why. _____

    _____

GO TO PART C IN YOUR TEXTBOOK.

Name ______________________________

A Story Items

1. What do nerves do?
   - carry messages
   - carry blood
   - carry oxygen

2. In which part of the man's body did Angela and Al start following the nerve? ______________________________

3. What did the pulses in the nerve feel like to Al?
   - big electric shocks
   - tiny electrical pulses
   - heavy pounding

4. Were there **more pulses** or **fewer pulses** when the man started tying his shoe? ______________________________

5. When the nerve was cut, how many pulses did the brain receive?

   ____

6. When would the nerves in your hand pulse faster—**when you're asleep** or **when you burn your hand?**

   ____

7. When the old man cut the nerve going from the brain to the hand, the man ______.
   - could not move his hand
   - could not feel his hand

8. When the old man cut the nerve going from the hand to the brain, the man ______.
   - could not move his hand
   - could not feel his hand

B Crossword Puzzle

numb	triceps
biceps	ice
ribs	skull
air	heart
lungs	oxygen
imagination	nerves
cerebrum	bones
steam	paralyzed

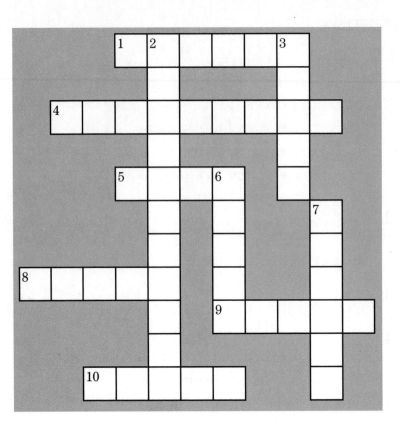

Across

1. The muscle that bends the arm is the ▨▨▨▨.

4. If you can't move a part of your body, that part is ▨▨▨▨.

5. Your ▨▨▨▨ protect your lungs and your heart.

8. Your ▨▨▨▨ pumps blood through your body.

9. If something hurt your ▨▨▨▨, you wouldn't be able to breathe.

10. Most muscles are attached to ▨▨▨▨.

Down

2. The part of your mind that can think of things that might happen is your ▨▨▨▨.

3. The gas form of water is ▨▨▨▨.

6. Your ▨▨▨▨ protects your brain.

7. Things can't burn without ▨▨▨▨.

GO TO PART C IN YOUR TEXTBOOK.

Name _____

Ⓐ

1. What happens to light when it goes through a magnifying glass?
     • It goes straight.
     • It goes faster.
     • It bends.

2. If you make a picture of a tree using a magnifying glass, the top

   of the tree will be at the _____ of the picture.

3. The eye is like a _____.

4. Where does light enter the eyeball?
                    • front   • side   • back

5. Where does the picture form?
                    • front   • side   • back

Ⓑ   **Story Items**

6. What do nerves that lead from the brain to the hand tell the hand?

   _____

7. What do nerves that lead from the hand to the brain tell the brain?

   _____

8. What is your backbone made of? _____

9. Name the bundle of nerves that goes up and down through the middle of your

   backbone. _____

10. What's strange about the bones in the backbone?
     • They are hollow.
     • They are solid.
     • They are soft.

11. When Al and Angela left the spinal cord, they entered the

_____.

12. What does your cerebrum do? _____

13. When Al and Angela first entered the brain, they were in a part that controls some things the body does. Name 2 of those things.

_____

_____

14. When Al and Angela moved up through the brain, they came to another part. Did that part have **more nerves** or **fewer nerves?**

_____

15. Name that part of the brain. _____

16. Which part of your **brain** works when you think about what you are

seeing? _____

GO TO PART D IN YOUR TEXTBOOK.

Name _____

A

1. Draw lines to show where the paths of light will go when they go through the lens.

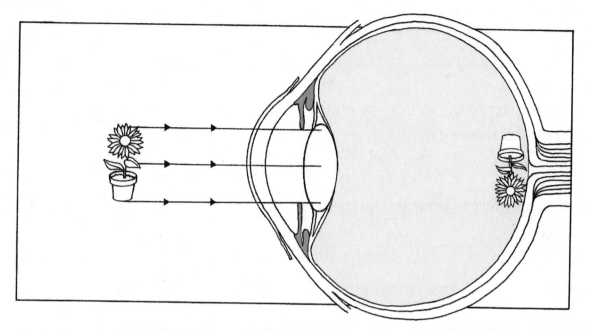

B **Story Items**

2. What did the old man do to scare the man?

_____

3. What happened to the nerves in the man's brain?
   - They pulsed more rapidly.
   - They pulsed more slowly.
   - They became cooler.

4. What did the nerves do after the lion disappeared?
   - They pulsed more rapidly.
   - They pulsed more slowly.
   - They became cooler.

5. The nerves from the eye go to the ▮▮▮▮ of the brain.
  - front   • side   • back

6. After Al and Angela left the brain, they went inside a great round chamber. What was that chamber?
  - the heart   • the eye   • the lungs

7. What is the name of the round window in the chamber?

   _____

8. On which part of the man's eye could Al and Angela see an image of what the man was looking at?
  - pupil   • retina   • lens

9. What was strange about the image they saw?

   _____

10. While Al and Angela were looking at the image, the man's shoes got bigger. Tell why. _____

   _____

Review Items

11. Name the bundle of nerves that goes up and down through the middle of your backbone. _____

12. What's strange about the bones in the backbone?
  - They are square.
  - They are hollow.
  - They are soft.

13. When you think, what part of your brain are you using?

   _____

GO TO PART D IN YOUR TEXTBOOK.

Name _____

A Story Items

1. The retina is covered with ▮▮▮▮.

   • nerves   • hair   • muscles

2. Each nerve in the retina feels the light and sends a message to the

   _____.

3. What would a person see if the big nerves from the eyes to the brain were

   cut? _____

4. What does the lens of your eye do to light?

   • bends it   • changes the colors   • magnifies it

5. What is the chamber inside the ear shaped like?

   • a box   • a spiral   • a circle

6. What is the inside of the ear's chamber lined with?

   _____

7. What is each hair inside the ear connected to?

   _____

8. When the hair moves, the nerve _____.

9. What happens if the hair vibrates very hard?
   • The nerve vibrates hard.
   • The nerve vibrates lightly.
   • The nerve feels colors.

10. What kinds of sounds are picked up in the biggest part of the chamber—

    high sounds or low sounds? _____

11. What kinds of sounds are picked up in the smallest part of the chamber—

    high sounds or low sounds? _____

Lesson 127   **103**

Write big or small to tell which part of your ear chamber would pick up each sound.

12. Big church bell _____

13. Low voice _____

14. Very high voice _____

15. High whistle _____

Review Items

16. Where does light enter the eyeball? _____

17. Where does the picture form? _____

18. The nerves from the eye go to the ▮▮▮ of the brain.
    - top   - back   - front

19. On which part of the man's eye could Al and Angela see an image of what the man was looking at?
    - lens   - retina   - pupil

20. The more water the glass has, the ▮▮▮ the sound it makes.
    - lower   - higher

21. **Underline** the glass that will make the lowest ring.

22. **Circle** the glass that will make the highest ring.

A   B   C   D   E   F

GO TO PART C IN YOUR TEXTBOOK.

Name _____

A Story Items

1. After the trip, the old man gave Al and Angela a book. What was the title of the book?

   _____

2. Why did he give the book to them? _____

   _____

3. Did the old man want the book back? _____

4. When will the old man give Al and Angela their test on the human body?

   _____

5. Was there snow on the ground when Al and Angela left the old man's store?

   _____

6. About how much snow was on the ground the next morning?

   _____

7. What did Al's mother ask him to do the next morning?

   _____

   _____

8. Who worked with Al? _____

Ⓑ Crossword Puzzle

spiral	numb	nerve	curved	blind
backbone	pupil	vessel	retina	hairs
paralyzed	four	cerebrum	red	black

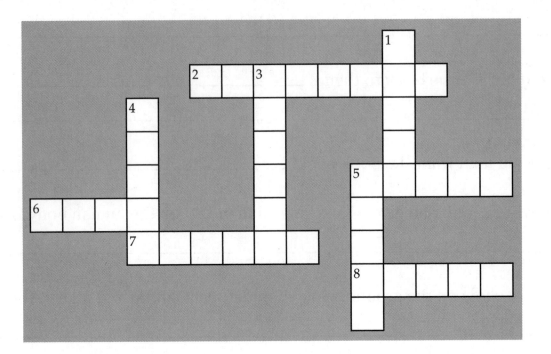

Across

2. The part of the brain that does the thinking is the ▉▉▉▉ .

5. Blood that does not have fresh oxygen is ▉▉▉▉ .

6. The heart has ▉▉▉▉ chambers.

7. The chamber inside the ear is shaped like a ▉▉▉▉ .

8. Something in your body that carries messages is a ▉▉▉▉ .

Down

1. The hole at the front of the eye is called the ▉▉▉▉ .

3. The part of the eye where pictures are formed is called the ▉▉▉▉ .

4. The ear's chamber is lined with ▉▉▉▉ .

5. A person who cannot see is ▉▉▉▉ .

GO TO PART C IN YOUR TEXTBOOK.

Name _____

Ⓐ

1. Look at the picture below. Is the side of the earth that's closest to the sun **in daylight** or **in darkness?** _____

2. Is the North Pole tilting **toward the sun** or **away from the sun?**

_____

3. So does this picture show our **summer** or our **winter?** _____

4. As the earth turns around, which person is in darkness all the time?

_____

5. Which person is in daylight all the time? _____

6. Write the letters of all the persons who are in daylight some of the time and

darkness some of the time. _____

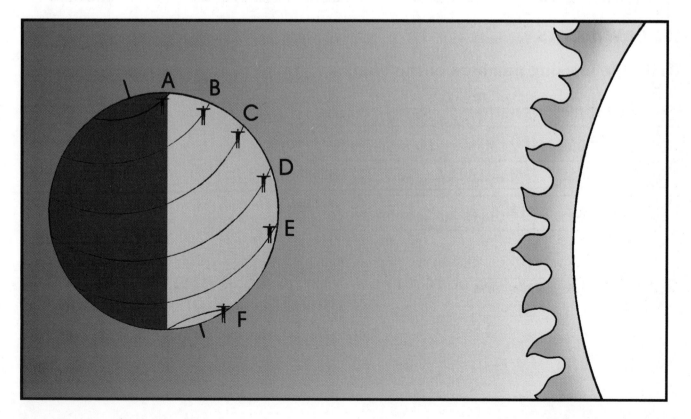

Lesson 129   **107**

B Story Items

7. Who made fun of Al in school? _____

8. How many questions were on the test that Al took in school? _____

9. What were most of the questions about?

   _____

10. Who did better on the test, Homer or Al? _____

11. What grade did Al get on the test? _____

12. How many questions did Angela miss?

    _____

13. Why didn't the old man give a test to Al and Angela?

    _____

    _____

Review Items

Write the missing numbers in the blanks.

___0___ feet	surface pressure
14. _____ feet	2 times surface pressure
15. _____ feet	3 times surface pressure
16. _____ feet	4 times surface pressure

GO TO PART D IN YOUR TEXTBOOK.

Name _____

A Story Items

1. Who decided where to go on the next trip?

   _____

2. Where did they go? _____

3. Why was it dark there?

   • It was winter.   • It was summer.

4. Why did Al's eyes start to burn? _____

   _____

5. What was the temperature at the North Pole?

   _____

6. What would that cold air do if you breathed too hard?

   _____

7. How much daylight is there during winter at the North Pole?

   _____

8. How much nighttime is there during the summer at the North

   Pole? _____

9. What season do we have when the North Pole tilts **toward** the

   sun? _____

10. What season do we have when the North Pole tilts **away from**

    the sun? _____

The old man made three tiny forms appear at the North Pole of the model Earth. Fill in the blanks with **dark** or **light.**

11. When it was **summer,** those forms stayed on the

_____ half of the earth.

12. When it was **winter,** those forms stayed on the

_____ half of the earth.

Review Items

13. Muscles are made up of tiny _____.

14. Blood vessels that are blue are filled with ████.

   • dark blood   • red blood

15. Muscle cells need _____ to work.

Use these words to answer the questions:

   • blood vessels that lead from the heart
   • blood vessels that lead to the heart

16. Which blood vessels are blue? _____

_____

17. Which blood vessels pound every time the heart beats? _____

_____

18. Which blood vessels do not pound? _____

_____

GO TO PART C IN YOUR TEXTBOOK.

Name _____

A Story Items

1. Do any two snowflakes look **exactly** alike? _____

2. How are all snowflakes the same? _____
_____

3. The old man made each snowflake as big as a
_____.

4. About how deep is the snow at the North Pole?
_____

5. What is under the snow at the North Pole?
_____

6. Which would be harder, snow that is **30 feet below** the top of a pile or snow that is **45 feet below** the top of the pile?
_____

7. How much land is under the North Pole? _____

8. How many states in the United States are as big as the North Pole?
_____

Review Items

9. The picture shows the sun and two balls. Fix up the balls so that half of each ball is in sunlight and half is in shadow.

10. **Write the letter** of the thing that travels the slowest. _____

11. **Write the letter** of the thing that travels the fastest. _____

   a. light   c. jet plane   e. rocket
   b. racing car   d. sound

12. Write the letters of the 5 things that are matter in the solid form.

   _____

13. Write the letters of the 4 things that are matter in the liquid form.

   _____

14. Write the letters of the 3 things that are matter in the gas form.

   _____

   a. rock   d. air   g. brick   j. wood
   b. smoke   e. water   h. tea   k. juice
   c. glass   f. milk   i. ice   l. steam

GO TO PART C IN YOUR TEXTBOOK.

Name _____

A

1. Draw lines to show where the paths of light will go through the lens.

2. Make an **F** in the box that shows where the film is.

3. Make an **L** in the box that shows where the lens is.

4. Make an **I** in the box that shows where the iris is.

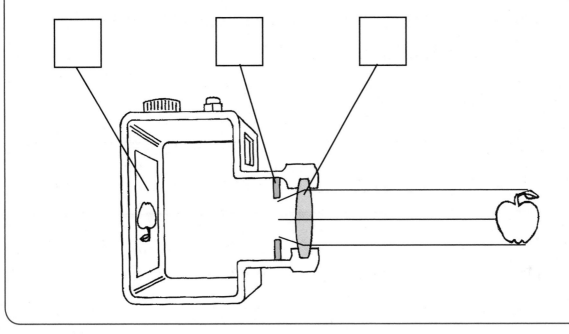

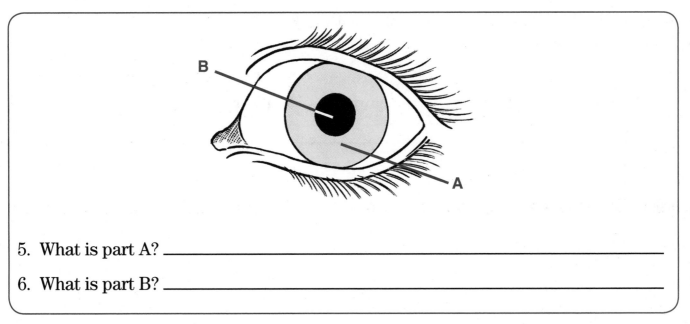

5. What is part A? _____

6. What is part B? _____

Lesson 133   **113**

B | Story Items

7. Fill in the blanks with **toward** or **away from.**

   During our winter, the North Pole tilts _____

   the sun, and the South Pole tilts _____ the sun.

8. Fill in the blanks with **dark** or **light.**

   During our winter, the North Pole is always _____

   and the South Pole is always _____.

9. How many hours does it take the sun to make a full circle at the poles?

   _____

10. What's under all the snow at the North Pole?

    _____

11. What's under the snow at the South Pole?

    _____

12. How many square miles is the land under the South Pole?

    • 1 million   • 5 hundred   • 5 million

13. About how deep is the snow at the South Pole?

    _____

14. Where is the snow deeper, at the North Pole or at the South Pole?

    _____

GO TO PART D IN YOUR TEXTBOOK.

Name _____

Ⓐ Story Items

1. A man gave Al and Angela each 5 dollars. Tell why.

   _____

   _____

2. Why was the man in a hurry to get home? _____

   _____

3. Why did Al want to get some more money? _____

   _____

4. About how deep was the snow in front of Al and Angela's house?

   _____

5. Why were the schools going to be closed the next day?

   _____

6. How had Al felt about school before the old man's trips?

   _____

7. How does Al feel about school now?

   _____

8. Why does he feel that way about school now?

   - He's a poor student.   - He's a good student.

   - He doesn't like school.

9. What is Angela and Al's last name? _____

10. What was the title of the book Al and Angela got in this story?

   _____

11. Who sent the book to them? _____

12. The ship named *Endurance* was stuck in ice at the

   _____.

13. How many men on that ship died? _____

14. What happened to Scott and the men with him?

   _____

15. What was strange about the food in Scott's camp when people found it fifty years later?

   _____

Review Items

16. What is each hair inside the ear connected to? _____

17. What kinds of sounds are picked up in the biggest part of the ear chamber—high sounds or low sounds?

   _____

18. What part of a camera bends the light that goes through it?

   _____

19. What part of a camera lets just enough light into the camera?

   _____

GO TO PART C IN YOUR TEXTBOOK.

Name _____

A

1. What are groups of baboons called? _____

2. Name an animal that looks something like a baboon but is much bigger.

   _____

3. Name an animal in the cat family that is the size of a big dog.

   _____

4. Name an animal in the whale family that some people think is the smartest.

   _____

5. Is that animal **warm-blooded** or **cold-blooded?**

   _____

6. How long ago did saber-toothed tigers disappear from the earth?

   _____

7. It is called a **saber-toothed tiger** because it had _____ like sabers.

B Story Items

8. What did Al want to read about at the library?

   _____

9. Was the library open? _____

10. Why were most of the stores closed? _____

_____

11. Where did Al and Angela go after breakfast?

_____

12. What did the old man want Al and Angela to do when they first

got to his store? _____

13. What did the old man give each of them for doing that?

_____

14. Did Al and Angela go to the store next door at the same time?

_____

15. What was the store next door filled with when Al went there?

_____

16. What was the store filled with when Angela went there?

_____

17. What did Al buy for his mother? _____

18. What did Al buy for Angela? _____

19. How much did **each present** cost? _____

20. What did Angela buy for Al? _____

21. What did Angela buy for her mother? _____

GO TO PART D IN YOUR TEXTBOOK.

Name _____

Ⓐ Story Items

1. Why did Al need the old man's trips when he first went to the store?

_____

_____

2. Why doesn't Al need the trips anymore? _____

_____

3. Who decided where to go on this trip?

_____

4. Where did they go? _____

5. About how many books were in the library?

   • 30 million   • 2 million   • 3 million

6. About how many of those books were about animals?

   • 3 thousand   • 3 hundred   • 3 million

7. What did Angela want to read about? _____

8. What was the brain of the library? _____

9. Did the old man order **one book** or **more than one?**

_____

10. What was the title of the first book the old man picked up from the table?

_____

11. Who will start reading from that book? _____

Lesson 136   **119**

Review Items

12. What is animal A? _____

13. What is animal B? _____

14. What is animal C? _____

15. What is animal D? _____

16. What is animal E? _____

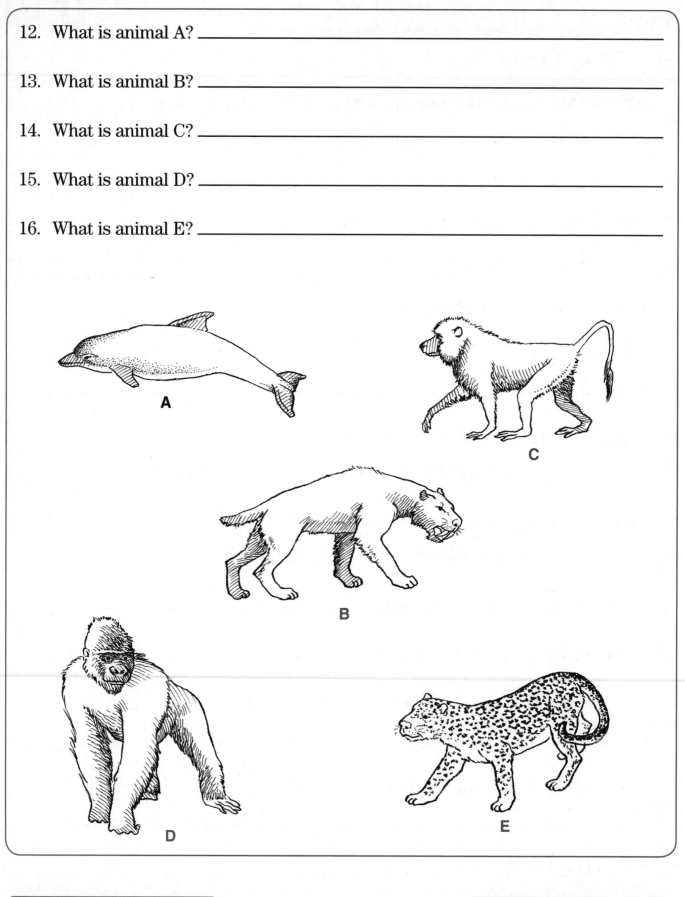

GO TO PART C IN YOUR TEXTBOOK.

Name _____

Ⓐ Story Items

1. What are the 2 kinds of seasons that Africa has?

   _____

2. What is the veld of Africa?

   _____

3. Name 3 kinds of animals that live on the veld in Africa.

   _____

4. Every day during the dry season, African animals go to a place where they
   don't usually fight. Name that place.

   _____

5. Did Al and Angela get to read the whole book about *Animals in Africa*?

   _____

6. What did the old man say they should do if they wanted to read more of the
   book? _____

   _____

7. Al and Angela read part of a book titled *How Animals Learn*. Which animal
   did that book say is next-smartest after humans?

   _____

8. Why do troops of baboons need lookouts? _____

   _____

retina	dolphin	iris	sunset	porpoise	pupil
lens	summer	shark	horizon	film
extend	Endurance	examine	south	north

Across

4. The part of a camera that bends the light is the ▆▆▆.

6. The place where the sky meets the ground is called the ▆▆▆.

7. Name an animal in the whale family that is very smart.

9. When the North Pole tilts toward the sun, we are having ▆▆▆.

Down

1. The pole at the bottom of the earth is called the ▆▆▆ Pole.

2. The part of a camera where pictures are formed is the ▆▆▆.

3. A ship that sank at the South Pole was named the ▆▆▆.

5. When you look at something very closely, you ▆▆▆ that thing.

8. The part of a camera that lets just enough light into the camera is the ▆▆▆.

GO TO PART C IN YOUR TEXTBOOK.

Name _____

A Story Items

1. Which dinosaur lived **earlier,** Plateosaurus or Tyrannosaurus?

   _____

2. About how long was Plateosaurus?

   _____

3. Why did Angela want to read about the solar system?

   _____

4. Did Al and Angela like the trip to the library as much as the other trips?

   _____

5. How many books about dinosaurs did the library have?

   - over 600   • over 1000   • less than 50

6. Dinosaurs lived during the _____.

7. How long ago did the Mesozoic begin?

   _____

8. Write 3 things that you would see in the jungle where the first dinosaurs lived.

   _____

   _____

9. The old man told Al and Angela, "You have to use your _____ to take a trip from a book."

10. Name 2 things that were different when Al and Angela left the old man's store.

_____

_____

11. What did Al do after dinner?

_____

12. What was special about the next day?

_____

Review Items

13. Which iris is right for taking a picture in a dark place? _____

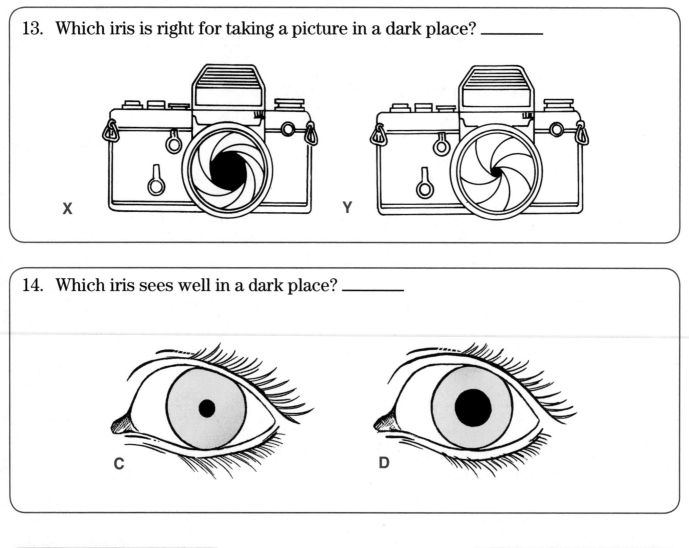

X   Y

14. Which iris sees well in a dark place? _____

C   D

GO TO PART C IN YOUR TEXTBOOK.

Name _____

A **Story Items**

1. What did Al's mother give Al for Christmas?

   _____

2. What did Al's family do after breakfast?

   _____

3. Did Al's mother think there was an Anywhere Street? _____

4. Was Al's mother right? _____

5. What was the **real** name of the street?

   _____

6. What kind of store did the old man have?

   _____

7. What kind of book did the old man give Al's mother?

   _____

8. What was the title of the book the old man gave Al and Angela?

   _____

Review Items

9. The dinosaurs lived in the _____.

10. Which dinosaur lived earlier, Plateosaurus or Tyrannosaurus?

   _____

11. About how long was Plateosaurus?

_____

12. Write 3 things that you would see in the jungle where the first dinosaurs
lived.

_____

_____

13. What is animal A? _____

14. What is animal B? _____

15. What is animal C? _____

16. What is animal D? _____

17. What is animal E? _____

A

E

C

B

D

GO TO PART C IN YOUR TEXTBOOK.

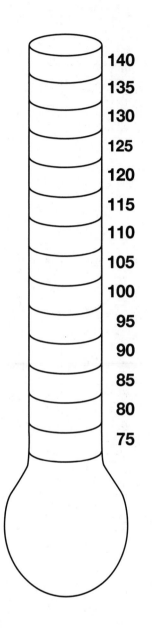

140
135
130
125
120
115
110
105
100
95
90
85
80
75

Fact Game Scorecards

Name

Lesson 80

1	2	3	4	5
6	7	8	9	10
11	12	13	14	15
16	17	18	19	20

Lesson 90

1	2	3	4	5
6	7	8	9	10
11	12	13	14	15
16	17	18	19	20

Lesson 100

1	2	3	4	5
6	7	8	9	10
11	12	13	14	15
16	17	18	19	20

Lesson 110

1	2	3	4	5
6	7	8	9	10
11	12	13	14	15
16	17	18	19	20

Lesson 120

1	2	3	4	5
6	7	8	9	10
11	12	13	14	15
16	17	18	19	20

Lesson 130

1	2	3	4	5
6	7	8	9	10
11	12	13	14	15
16	17	18	19	20

Lesson 140

1	2	3	4	5
6	7	8	9	10
11	12	13	14	15
16	17	18	19	20